World's most famous representation of "Justice"

Explanatory note: This representation of Lady Justice with her eyes wide open stands atop London's Old Bailey, scene of many famous jury criminal trials including that of William Penn and William Mead in 1670 (then Newgate prison, see page 86 for details of the Penn trial.)

THE JURY

Tool of Kings
Palladium of Liberty

LLOYD E. MOORE

CINCINNATI
THE W.H. ANDERSON COMPANY

Copyright © 1973

By

THE W.H. ANDERSON COMPANY

Library of Congress Catalog Card Number: 73-85855

CONTENTS

Foreword

The institution of the jury — the subject of this book — is as timely as it is hoary. For a considerable period of time, the jury system has been the focal point of discussion and debate by both legal and non-legal writers. Thus, Mark Twain said: "The jury system puts a ban upon intelligence and honesty, and a premium upon ignorance, stupidity, and perjury. It is a shame that we must continue to use a worthless system because it was good a thousand years ago." Likewise, Dean Griswold observed:

> But jury trial, at best, is the apotheosis of the amateur. Why should anyone think that twelve persons brought in from the street, selected in various ways, for their lack of general ability, should have any special capacity for deciding controversies between persons.

On the other hand, G. K. Chesterton has offered the following defense of the jury:

> Our civilization has decided, and very justly decided that determining the guilt or innocence of men is a thing too important to be trusted to trained men. If it wishes for light upon that awful matter, it asks men who know no more law than I know, but who can feel the things I felt in a jury box. When it wants a library catalogued, or the solar system discovered, or any trifle of that kind, it uses up its specialists. But when it wishes anything done that is really serious, it collects twelve of the ordinary men standing about. The same thing was done, if I remember right, by the Founder of Christianity.

In a similar vein, Dean Roscoe Pound concluded that "jury lawlessness is the great corrective of law in its actual administration."

Interest in this subject has been rekindled by the attacks which have recently been leveled against the adversary system, including the proliferation of no-fault schemes. Many of these proposals would abolish the jury as a justice-dispensing institution. Hence, it is imperative that there be enlightened discussion of the relative merits and deficiencies of this venerable system which the United States Supreme Court has aptly characterized (in at least criminal cases) as being "fundamental to the American scheme of justice."

Mr. Moore is to be commended for providing us with this book which is a telescope into time. He approaches the issues with a wide focus and gives us the benefits of historical insights and perspectives. This book illuminates the area and chases the mid-Victorian shadows and myths which previously dominated discussion.

William Schwartz
General Director
Association of Trial Lawyers of America
Cambridge, Massachusetts
July, 1973

Preface

That a sophisticated people would leave decisions affecting fortune, honor and life to a fixed number of individuals, selected at random, without regard to intelligence, experience or education would seem to defy rational explanation.

The reasons lie in history. The first records of institutions ancestral to the jury are coeval with history itself. The ancient Mediterranean civilizations and the Germanic tribes had groups of laymen who participated in judgment. From these early sources to the modern trial jury there are great gaps, but even biological evolution seldom has a complete chain.

From the time of Henry II of England, the record is reasonably clear but no less interesting. We find that our ancestors were tortured to force them to submit to trial by jury. Jurors were starved into rendering verdicts. Distinctive types of juries evolved to try the cases of aliens and business cases. Occasionally, jurors risked their own fortunes by insisting on rendering a verdict in accordance with their consciences and against the direction of judges who were under the influence of the crown.

Revolutionary America took the jury to its heart as a weapon in its struggle with the mother country. The power of the jury increased and was practically unchallenged in nineteenth century America. It is only in the last half of the present century that signs are appearing that indicate the long story of the jury may be coming to an end. The jury's most serious competitors are arbitration and trial by judge alone. Of these two, trial by judge poses the jury's most serious threat. It is for this reason and for the reason that most objections to judges apply to arbitrators that the last chapter is devoted to a comparison of judges and jury trial. Trial experience and historical research have left the writer with the conviction that the quality of justice and liberty itself will suffer if the role of jury trial is further diminished. It may be that the reader will disagree with this conclusion but still find the story of jury trial to be a fascinating one.

Lloyd E. Moore
Chesapeake, Ohio
June 23, 1973

Acknowledgments

My special thanks for assistance in the preparation of this book are extended to the library staff of the Institute For Advanced Legal Studies of the University of London, the libraries of the British Museum, the Middle Temple, the Law Society and the libraries of the Royal Borough of Kensington and Chelsea. My thanks are also extended to my law partners, John Wolfe and Dennis Boll, who kept our law business running while I worked on the book. I am indebted to William Schwartz, General Director of the American Trial Lawyers Association, and to Judge Robert L. McBride, author of *The Art of Instructing the Jury* and common pleas judge of Montgomery County, Ohio for their kindness in reading the manuscript and making useful suggestions. Instrumental in the publication of this book was the interest of John L. Skirving, President of W.H. Anderson Company, whose encouragement and friendship are highly valued. Finally, I am grateful for the assistance of my wife, Marilyn, who corrected and typed the manuscript.

I
Creation of the Gods

i

Odysseus stole the statue of Pallas Athena from the Trojans, and without this protection, the Greeks were thus able to destroy the city. Upon his homecoming, Agamemnon, commander-in-chief of the Greeks, was murdered by his wife as a solution to her marital problems. This drastic action by Clytemnestra was distressing to her children; so acute was the reaction of her offspring that Orestes, at the urging of his sister and with the approval of Apollo, killed his mother and her latest lover.

This sequence of events could have ended at this point if the Greeks had not held strong views on matricide. The local citizens were supported in their revulsion at Orestes' deadly revenge by three demigods, known collectively as the Eumenides or Furies. The people and spirits gave Orestes no rest, and he finally sought refuge at Athens where Pallas Athena called together twelve citizens of Athens to try him on the charge of matricide. Apollo, to his credit, was the chief witness and advocate for Orestes, while the Eumenides pressed for prosecution.

This first jury trial of a mortal*, having taken place over three thousand years ago, could well have ended in a hung jury, as there were six votes for conviction and six for acquittal. However, Pallas Athena, in her belief that the better part of justice was mercy, broke the tie and voted for acquittal. This story of the founding of the jury by the patron goddess of wisdom is most clearly set forth in the play *Eumenides* by Aeschylus, who died in 456 B.C.[1]

---

* The very first trial held on the Areopagus was that which tried the god Ares for the murder of Halirrhothius, son of Poseidon. The jury of twelve gods split six to six, and Ares was acquitted. The New Century Classical Handbook, Catherine B. Avery, editor, Appleton-Century-Crofts, Inc. (New York, 1962), p. 149.

We are on firmer historical ground when we come to the time of Solon, who most probably lived in the last of the seventh and the first part of the sixth century B.C. History tells us this lawgiver reconstituted the court known as the Areopagus (the tribunal described above by Aeschylus) and another court, the Ephetae.[2] This latter court was composed of fifty-one men above the age of fifty and of noble birth. The membership of the Areopagus was drawn from those citizens who had held the office of archon, nine of whom combined to rule the city-state of Athens.[3] It should not be thought that the lateness of this era in history precludes the historical validity of the trial of Orestes as described by Aeschylus. The Areopagus was known to have existed long before the time of Solon, but he was simply the first to definitely arrange and legalize its constitution.[4]

Certainly, the Areopagus and the Ephetae do not appear particularly democratic in their membership when compared to the modern American jury, but there is more to the Athenian story. Existing along with those two courts was the general assembly of Athenian citizens which held the power of appeal over the other courts.[5] By 450 B.C., the supremacy of the assembly was established in all civil and criminal trials. Any Athenian citizen of the age of thirty or older, who was not indebted to the state and whose civil rights had not been forfeited, was eligible to serve, the members being chosen by lot. The assemblies were of varying sizes, ranging from 200 to 1,500, with one member always being added to prevent a tie.[6] There was even a mention of one jury in the time of Demosthenes with 2,000 members, plus the usual tie-breaker.[7] The number varied with the importance of the case,[8] and if the party prosecuting failed to get the fifth part of the votes, he was subject to a fine.[9]

The jury, or *dikasteria* as it was called, met in an area enclosed by rope in the face of the sun.[10] The jurors rendered their verdict on both facts and law, voting in secret and their judgment was not subject to appeal. The magistrate was merely a chairman responsible for order. Pericles also introduced pay for jury service.[11] When the oligarchy seized power during the period from 411 to 404 B.C., they abolished the jury, but the democratic party immediately restored it on their return to power.[12]

According to John Pettingal, the jury of the Athenians was brought to Rome by the Decemvirs who had been sent to Athens to investigate the laws of Solon around 451-50 B.C.[13] As described by Pettingal, the system provided for Judices (the jurors) who were chosen once a year to try criminal cases. Out of the entire number, 81 were chosen for a particular trial. Of these, 15 were challenged by each side, leaving fifty-one to decide the case under the supervision of a praetor or Judex Quaestionis, who received the vote and declared the verdict.[14] It was Gracchus who, about 122 B.C., engineered the passage of a statute which transferred the membership of the jury from the senatorial class to the equestrian class.[15] The judging was finally restored to the Senate by Sulla in the year 70 B.C.[16] The size of the jury, however, varied, and in the time of Cicero ranged from 51 to 75 members.[17]

The Roman Judices determined the guilt or innocence of the accused, resolving both questions of fact and of law, and could acquit or condemn regardless of the evidence.[18] The Judices voted on tablets which were marked with either a "C", "A", or the letters "N.L." which, respectively, stood for Absolvo, Condemno and Non Liquet, the latter being their verdict when in doubt.[19]

It is the theory of Pettingal that when the Romans subdued Gaul and, under the rule of Claudius (41-50 A.D.), reduced England to a province, they brought their form of the jury with them. The Romans were to remain in England, for the most part, until the fall of Rome to Alaric in 410 A.D.,[20] or possibly until 448 A.D.[21] Evidence has been found that the Burgundians of southeast France had the Roman form of the jury in the fifth century A.D.[22] From this, it is reasoned that either the idea of the jury survived in England from Roman days, or was brought over by the Angles and Saxons, emigrating to England around 430 A.D. at the request of the Britons to help control the Picts and Scots.[23] The result of this "good neighbor policy" was that the Angles and Saxons forcibly uprooted Briton civilization, dispersing their hosts into exile in Wales.[24]

Although this account of the Greek and Roman origin of the English jury is considered fanciful by most serious histo-

rians, the possibility of a residual Roman influence is not entirely discounted. Pollock and Maitland, citing Brunner, leave
open the possibility that the Frankish inquisitio, an ancestor of
the jury, was influenced by the Roman procedures.[25] Jerome
Frank was able to say in 1949 that the "germ" of the idea was
perhaps borrowed from fifth century Roman procedure.[26]

Having gone that far, we might as well agree with Pettingal
that the Greeks and perhaps even the Egyptians had a role in
the formation of the jury. The Egyptians had a jury (kenbet) of
eight members, four from each side of the Nile, which tried minor charges against workmen in the necropolises. A fellow
workman presided. This jury existed almost 4,000 years ago —
that is, about 750 years before the trial of Orestes. The Myceneans had trade missions in Egypt by at least the fourteenth
century B.C.[26], and it is possible that the idea of judgment by
one's peers may have been passed by the Myceneans to the
Greeks, and so on, as Pettingal supposed.

ii

Odin, the man who became a god,[27] led a Sythian people
from the east (perhaps, considering language similarities, from
near India[28]) and settled in Sweden, reputedly becoming the
earliest settlers of northern Europe.[29] On the authority of the
Edda, a collection of Icelandic theogony and cosmogony edited
by Snorri Sturluson at the beginning of the thirteenth century,[30] "Odin ordained twelve Asagods to adjudge all causes in
the metropolis of Asgard."[31] We are to assume that Odin himself presided as lawman or judge at this court of assessors or jurors.[32] It is also probable that he introduced trial by battle as
well.[33]

Be that as it may, this form of jury trial is the oldest "legal",
as opposed to "customary", mode of trial known among the
Scandinavians.[34] When historical records were first available
around 800 A.D., the jury was already in existence.[35] At this

early time, trial by battle was considered the nobler mode of trial, with the jury being reserved for the weak, the aged and women.[36] About the time Christianity was introduced by Bishop Poppo in Jutland (950 A.D.),[37] the jury became more popular and was the normal but not exclusive mode of trial among the northmen for the next two and one half centuries.[38] Besides trial by jury and battle, they also used trial by wager of law[39] and by ordeal[40], along with the rest of northern Europe.

The number of jurors on Scandinavian juries also varied. Traditionally, twelve was the most popular number, although the Norway Thing (assembly of the people), held on the Isle of Guley, had 36 jurors. The Scandinavians had no principle of unanimity, the causes usually being decided by a mere majority.[41]

The code of Magnus, King of Norway, gives some idea of the Scandinavian jury trial. It was promulgated in 1274 and reads in part as follows:

> The thing shall last so long as the lawman chooses, and during such time as he, with the consent of the jury, deems necessary for adjudging the causes which there are to be heard. Their number is three times twelve; their nomination must be so managed that some fit men be chosen from every district. Those who are chosen to be jurors shall, before they enter the court, swear on oath after the following form:
> "I protest before God that I will give such a vote in every cause, as well on the side of the plaintiff as defendant, as I consider most just in the sight of God, according to law and my conscience; And I shall always do the same whenever I shall be chosen as juror."
> This oath, every man is to swear before he enters the court, the first time he serves on a jury, but not a second time, though he should be chosen. Every man must go fasting into court, and make his appearance there while the sun is in the east, and remain in the court till noon. No man must bring any drink into court, neither, for sale nor in any other way. If those

who are outside the sacred cords make there such
noise and disturbance that the jurors are prevented
from hearing or those from pleading who have obtained leave from the lawman and the jurors, they
shall pay a fine of one silver, when detected and convicted, having been previously admonished.

Those who are chosen to serve as jurors shall
judge according to law in all causes that in a lawful
manner and course are hither (that is, to Gula-thing)
appealed. But in all cases that the code does not decide
that is to be considered law which all the jurors agree
upon. But if they disagree, the lawman prevails with
those who agree with him; unless the king with the
advice of the most prudent men shall otherwise decide.[42]

This code gave the lawman more power than he had had previously when he was only adviser.[43] The jurors on this island
were surrounded by cords held by staves as in Greece.[44]

Provisions were made in Sweden for twelve men to be selected in every lawman's district for the purpose of seeking out
lawbreakers. These were sworn to "... not make any man guilty
who is innocent, nor any man innocent who is guilty." Decision
was by at least seven of their number. The Swedish jury combined the functions of the grand and petty juries.[45] In Iceland,
twelve judges or jurors tried cases in the first instance with appeal allowable to a court with thirty-six judges which met on
midsummer's day.[46] Juries in Scandinavia generally fell into disuse after the fourteenth century, but there is record of a jury
being used in Sweden as late as 1665 A.D.[47]

Most modern authorities do not claim the Scandinavian jury
as an ancestor of the English jury.[48] Reeves, however, claimed
that it came to them through the Normans[49], as does Repp.[50] A
more direct route was through the Danes. Aethelred the Unready promulgated a law in 997 A.D. which was applicable only
to the Danish district of England. It provided for a moot (assembly) to be held in every wapentake (hundred), during which the
twelve eldest thegns of the community were required to swear
upon a relic that the reeve put into their hands, that they would

accuse no one innocent, nor conceal any guilty person. This early accusing jury did not seem to have any immediate descendants, and we must find another source for the English jury.[51]

iii

The analogies of the English jury with the institutions of the Greeks, Romans and the Scandinavians do not exhaust the instances of comparison. We will look more closely at the chief example, the Frankish, in the next chapter. There are other suggestions of origin of the English jury, however, that are of interest and to which we will now turn.

It is not surprising, considering that in the eighteenth century the jury survived only in England and its dependencies, that the English conceived of the jury as being indigenous to English soil. Writing in 1682 A.D., the anonymous author of *A Guide to English Juries* said, "Of what date juries be, is the same to say, as when was England first inhabited...."[52] In a work published in 1752, it was said that the jury's "... antiquity is beyond the reach of record of history."[53] In a supposed dialogue between a barrister and a juryman in 1680, the barrister, when asked how long trial by jury had been in use, replied, "Even time out of mind; so long, that our best historians cannot date the original of the institution, being indeed contemporary with the nation itself .... That juries ... were in use among the Britons, the first inhabitants of this island, appears by the ancient monuments and writings of that nation..."[54] The Welsh claim that their Bishop Aser Whenenensis brought the jury to the attention of King Alfred, who adopted it from them for England.[55] Actually, if all that is required of an ancestor to the modern jury is that it contain the laity as judges, the ancient druids, who preceded the Romans in Britain, would qualify.[56]

Jerusalem is one of the more unexpected locations as a source of the jury. In 1099 A.D., the crusaders captured Jerusalem from the Saracens. The laws they established were generally modeled on the laws of France, whose soldiers made up a majority of the crusaders. Godfrey, Duke of Bouellon, was made

king of Jerusalem. He established two secular courts in Jerusalem, the High Court where he was the chief justice, and the
Court of Burgesses where the judges were townspeople. In the
Burgesses' Courts, an officer (vescomete) presided over a court
composed of himself and twelve jurors. The jurors, however appointed, sat permanently, but it was not necessary that the
entire twelve should sit at one time; two or three were all that
were required. If the accused objected to the court's decision,
he could charge it with falsehood and challenge the entire
bench to mortal combat. If he did not fight them all, one after
the other, or if he did not vanquish them all in a single day, he
was beheaded in the first instance or hanged in the second.
There is no record of a successful appeal. For a time, some
looked upon this as the original jury.[57]

Even the Russians, not surprisingly, have some claim as the
jury's founding ancestor. In the oldest law of the Russians, it is
said, "...The thief who denies his guilt and every debtor who re-
fuses to pay must prove his innocence before twelve men."[58] It
is possible that since the Normans were instrumental in the
founding of the Russian nation, this tribunal may be derived
from Scandinavian sources. It is certain, however, that this and
other remote examples have only a coincidental resemblance to
the English jury and did not influence its development.

With the foregoing history and mythology serving as an introduction to the story of the jury, it would be well at this point
to see what can be done about a definition of the jury itself, so
that the reader will have a basis from which to organize the material. Forsyth defined it thus: "...the jury consists of a body of
men taken from the community at large, summoned to find the
truth of disputed facts, who are quite distinct from the judges or
court."[59]

Kalven and Zeisel, in *The American Jury*, said,

"It [the jury] recruits a group of twelve laymen, chosen at random from the widest population; it convenes
them for the purpose of the particular trial; it entrusts
them with great official powers of decision; it permits
them to carry on deliberations in secret and to report
out their final judgment without giving reasons for it;

and, after their momentary service to the state has
been completed, it orders them to disband and return
to private life."[60]

Pollock and Maitland put it more simply, "...a body of
neighbors is summoned by some public officer to give upon oath
a true answer to some question."[61] If this last definition is kept
in mind, it will be seen why the Franks have been taken as the
starting point of the English jury by Brunner and others.

Chapter I footnotes

1. *Aeschyli Eumenides*, translated by Jernard Drake (MacMillan and Co., 1853).

2. *Id.* at p. 58.

3. *Ibid.*

4. Drake, *op. cit.* at note 1, at p. 67.

5. *A History of Lay Judges*, John P. Dawson (Harvard Univ. Press, 1960), p. 11.

6. *Ibid.*

7. *An Enquiry Into the Use and Practice of Juries Among the Greeks and Romans*, John Pettingal (London, 1769), pp. 29, 36.

8. *Id.* at p. 36.

9. Pettingal, *op. cit,* at note 7, at p. 30.

10. Pettingal, *op. cit.* at note 7, at pp. 33, 45.

11. Dawson, *op. cit.* at note 5, at pp. 11-12.

12. Dawson, *op. cit.* at note 5, at p. 12.

13. Pettingal, *op. cit.* at note 7, at p. 139.

14. Pettingal, *op. cit.* at note 7, at p. 135.

15. Dawson, *op. cit.* at note 5, at pp. 16-17.

16. Dawson, *supra*, p. 18. *op. cit.* at note 5, at p. 18.

17. *Ibid.*

18. *History of Trial by Jury*, William Forsyth (John Parker and Son, London, 1852), pp. 12-13.

19. *Id.*, at p. 12.

20. Pettingal, *op. cit.* at note, 7, at pp. 140-58.

21. *History of the English Law*, John Reeves (Reed and Hunter, London, 1814), I-p. 2.

22. Pettingal, *op. cit.* at note 7, at preface p. vii.

23. *Id.* at I. pp. 2-3; *op. cit.* at note 7, at p. 158.

24. Reeves, *supra, op. cit.* at note 22, at p. 3.

25. *The History of English Law*, Sir Frederick Pollock and Frederic William Maitland (Cambridge Univ. Press, 2nd Ed., 1898), I-p. 141.

26. *Courts on Trial*, Jerome Frank (Princeton Univ. Press, 1949), p. 108.

* 26a *Tutankhamen*, Christiane Desroches-Noblecourt (Penguin Books Ltd, Harmondsworth, England, translated by Claude, first ed. 1963), pp. 34, 106.

27. *A Historical Treatise on Trial by Jury*, Thorl. Gudn. Repp (Thomas Clark, Edinburgh, 1832) p. 16.

28. *Id.*, at p. 69.

29. Repp, *op. cit.* at note 27, at pp. 16-17.

30. Repp, *op. cit.* at note 27, at p. 72.

31. Repp, *op. cti.* at note 27, at p. 6.

32. Repp, *op. cit.* at note 27, at p. 75.

33. Repp, *op. cit.* at note 27, at p. 17.

34. Repp, *op. cit.* at note 27, at p. 20.

35. Repp, *op. cit.* at note 27, at p. 5.

36. Repp, *op. cit.* at note 27, at p. 9.

37. *History of Trial By Jury*, William Forsyth (John W. Parker and Son, London, 1852), p. 17.

38. Repp, *op. cit.* at note 27, at p. 17.

39. Repp, *op. cit.* at note 27, at pp. 100-02.

40. Repp, *op. cit.* at note 27, at p. 13.

41. Repp, *op. cit.* at note 27, at pp. 76-79.

42. Forsyth, *op. cit.* at note 18, at pp. 18-21.

43. *Ibid.*

44. Repp, *op. cit.* at note 27, at p. 47.

45. Forsyth, *op. cit.* at note 18, at pp. 22-24.

46. Forsyth, *op. cit.* at note 18, at p. 32.

47. Repp, *op. cit.* at note 27, at pp. 76-79.

48. Pollock and Maitland, *op. cit.* at note 25, at I-p. 140; *A Preliminary Treatise on Evidence*, James Bradley Thayer (Sweet and Maxwell, London, 1898), p. 129; *The Origin of Juries*, Heinrich Brunner (Berlin, 1872). (The copy read by the writer was a handwritten translation at the Institute of Advanced Legal Studies, University of London, translated, W.H. Humphreys, 1951; see pp. 29-30 for his claim of Frankish origin); *A History of Lay Judges*, John P. Dawson (Harvard Univ. Press, 1960), pp. 119-20. The author accepts the Frankish origin as by Brunner tempered with the observation that this may not be true of the Jury of accusation; "The Origin and Development of Trial by Jury", H.H. Grooms, 26 Ala. Law 162 (1965).

49. *History of the English Law*, John Reeves, Esq. (London, 1814), p. 84.

50. Repp, *op. cit.* at note 27, at pp. 48, 162.

51. Pollock and Maitland, *op. cit.* at note 25, at I-142-43.

52. *A Guide to Juries*, By a Person of Quality, attributed by Forsyth to Lord Somers (London, 1682), p. 1.

53. *The Complete Juryman*, anonymous (London, 1752), p. 3.

54. *The English Man's Right*, Sir John Hawles, 6th Ed. (London, 1771, being a reprint of the 1680 ed.), p. 4.

55. Brunner, *op. cit.* at note 48, at p. 13.

56. Brunner, *op. cit.* at note 48, at pp. 21-22.

57. Forsyth, *op. cit.* at note 18, at pp. 114-120.

58. Brunner, *op. cit.* at note 48, at p. 25.

59. Forsyth, *op. cit.* at note 18, at p. 8.

60. *The American Jury*, Harry Kalven, Jr. and Hans Zeisel (Little, Brown & Co., Boston, 1966) p. 3.

61. Pollock and Maitland, *op. cit.* at note 25, at I-138.

II
Charlemagne's Inquisitio

By 253 A.D., the Franks occupied extensive holdings in Europe, including the Netherlands and most of Gaul. Much of their success in conquest was attributable to the rule of the Merovingian family, whose rulers formed a strong central government by the seventh century,[1] and continued in power until they were replaced by the Carolingians in 751 A.D.[2] Charlemagne (Charles the Great) became king of the Franks in 768 A.D. and created the greatest empire that western Europe had seen since the fall of Rome. By 780 A.D., Charlemagne had established these reforms in the Frankish legal system: (1) Ordinary freemen were relieved of the burden of attending court. (Germanic peoples had generally conducted their trials through an assembly of the people whose approval of the judgment was necessary to validate the result); (2) A permanent group of lawfinders was appointed by the central authority with a vague requirement of local consent. This was intended to make the law more uniform by giving one group of justices greater decision-making power[3]; (3) An "inquisitio" was established for the resolution of disputed factual situations in which the crown had an interest.[4]

By 800 A.D., the decision in the ordinary courts was decided by the royal presiding officer and the law-finder (a local legal expert) alone, without the consent of any popular assembly. The administrative officer of a royal district, the count, was also authorized to give judgment in less important matters without reference to an assembly. General meetings of the people were held in conjunction with the courts three times a year, and at these hearings the assent of the assembly was required.[5]

Our interest in Charlemagne's legal reforms is the inquisitio. Brunner defines this institution as follows:

> Its distinctive feature consists in the fact that the judge may summon, at his discretion, a number of men from the neighborhood in whom he can assume a

13

knowledge of the matter in question, and demand
from them the promise to declare the truth upon the
question to be submitted by him. After the promise
comes the judicial putting of the question, "Inquisitio."[6]

The inquisitio of the Franks had its accusatory aspects
which anticipated our modern grand jury and its civil aspects,
which was a mode of proof by inquisition or interrogation. The
next step in the evolution of the trial jury was the Anglo-Norman jury of proof. The jurors themselves were the witnesses
and they were the mode of proof, as they were in the ordeal,
deed, or compurgation. The final step in the jury's development
was the judgment jury which came into being in England in the
fourteenth century. In this last step, the jury, instead of being a
mode of proof, chose between the proofs or evidence offered by
the parties.[7]

It is important at this point to refer once more to Pollock
and Maitland's definition of the jury, written in 1898: "...a body
of neighbors is summoned by some public officer to give upon
oath a true answer to some question."[8] If the reader will keep
this definition in mind and heed Edmund Burke's suggestion not
to expect to find that modern juries "... have jumped, like Min-
erva, out of the head of Jove in complete armor..."[9], he will be
better able to analyze the beginnings of the jury as found in the
inquisitio.

The inquisitio was a royal prerogative, and available only
upon royal command.[10] At first, it was generally used only in
fiscal affairs of the crown, but gradually the right to use the inquisitio was extended to the church.[11] In a capitulary (ordinance)
of Louis the Pious in 826 A.D., the church gained the privilege
of calling the inquisitio for any land question concerning church
property ceded to the crown. (This did not hold true for land
transferred to the church from the state.)[12] However, in 829
A.D., this prerogative was extended to the church with respect
to any property where it could demonstrate thirty years of un-
broken possession. Generally itinerant judges (missi) had the authority to use the inquisitio,[13] but an ordinary or local judge did
not.[14] Royal mandates were issued to agents of the crown di-

recting them to undertake inquisitios,[15] although these agents might be ordinary judges.[16]

An ordinary judge could conduct an inquisitio when: (1) a party entitled to it demanded it; (2) the king entrusted the count (administrative head of the county) with the privilege of jurisdiction. (This was rare in the early years of the Frankish administration; i.e., from 780-830); (3) a Jew was a party. (Under formal witness proof, a Jew needed six Christians to prove a case against a Christian, whereas a Christian only needed three Jews and three Christians to prove a case against a Jew); and (4) the party was a person entitled to the special protection of the king by reason of unfitness to participate in the ordinary proof; e.g., orphans, widows, and incompetents.[17]

The royal mandate ordering an inquisitio to be undertaken was sometimes delivered by a royal agent (missus who may or may not have been a judge) to the officer charged with holding the hearing.[18] At other times the party who had petitioned for the inquisitio delivered the mandate to the presiding officer.[19] Thus, in 890 A.D., Bishop Gilbert complained to the king and obtained an inquisitio-mandate and laid it before the judge.[20] As it would be inconvenient for a large number of witnesses to travel a long distance, the officer charged with holding the inquisitio generally went to the place where the majority of the witnesses lived.[21]

The officer undertaking the inquisitio chose his witnesses from the neighborhood where it could be assumed they would have knowledge of the matter in dispute. Only the most trustworthy, the best of the freemen, were chosen. The number of witnesses was largely within the discretion of the officer. A minimum number was never fixed.[22] There is an example of an inquisitio with 200 members,[23] but usually the number of members would range between thirteen and 66.[24] For example, 20 members were selected to decide hunting and fishing rights in Abersee.[25] Under a mandate of Charlemagne issued in favor of the church of Lorsch, 14 men whose names were recorded were appointed. Except in an exceptional case, the number of the members usually would not fall below that level for formal witness proof.[26] (In like manner, the number 12 probably came to

be the standard number of members for the English trial jury.)
The officer had the authority to enforce the attendance of the
witness-members of the inquisitio.[27] The Frankish people may
have been an intemperate lot, accounting for the capitulary of
Charlemagne forbidding anyone under the influence of liquor to
plead his cause.[28] Pettingal suggests that this is the origin of the
later English prohibition against juries having meat or drink.

The oaths taken by the members of the inquisitio were
promissory; that is, they promised to speak the truth without
reference to the subject of the dispute.[29] After the oath was administered, the question was stated by the officer in charge. He
could put the question to them one at a time or all at once,[30] and
the witnesses could give testimony helpful to either side.[31] This
procedure contrasts sharply with the formal witness proof of
the Franks, where a party selected his own witnesses who were
questioned only as to identity. In formal proof, the witnesses
took an assertive oath; that is, they swore that the oath of the
party who called them was true.[32] Some jurymen were exempted from taking the oath; e.g., priests could be employed in
the inquisitio, but not generally in witness proof. They therefore were not sworn but made a declaration according to the
vows of their particular priestly office.[33]

A party before an inquisitio had no burden of proof. In an
earlier time, although the presiding officer had the authority to
undertake the inquisitio, he needed special authority to decide
the matter in dispute.[34] But, in civil matters the inquisitio came
to be a means of proof by which a party could obtain a conclusive judgment.[35] The parties could not challenge the verdict
of an inquisitio by resort to a duel, as was the practice in formal
proof,[36] but the court could order the ordeal against a member
of the panel suspected of perjury. There were benefits in finding
for the crown, as was to be true of later English panels. In 802
A.D. Charlemagne decreed protection for members of inquisitios that found in favor of the crown. But, in 845 A.D.,
there was a verdict against the crown in favor of a church, and
church revenues was restored.

If the members of the panel were able to reach no definite
conclusion, another jury might be ordered, although the mem-

bers of the first panel that had definite information might be retained. (This is similar to the early English technique called "afforcement.") If the second inquisitio produced no result, the parties were relegated to formal proof.

There were complaints about jury duty even during this period. The procedure was regarded with suspicion, and the people strove to limit its employment. In 855-56 A.D., King Louis held court in Pavia, and his subjects complained of being overburdened by the jury duty which had been imposed. The king promised that its use would be limited to the levels that had existed during the days of the early Frankish administrations.[37]

This, then, was the earliest ancestor of the modern trial jury. That it existed in Neustria (the Frankish name for the province of Normandy) is certain. The circuit of the itinerant judges had been re-established there by Charles the Bald in 853 A.D.[38] However, the Northmen raided the northwest coast of France in the second half of the ninth century, and they established permanent settlements in the lower Seine in the last decade of that century. After having gained a reputation as an adventurer in Scottish and Irish raids, Rollo the Walker, son of Rognvald of Norway, came to the lower Seine settlements where he was the outstanding leader by 911 A.D. In that year he defeated the forces of Charles the Simple, and, by the resulting treaty, most of modern Normandy was ceded to the Northmen. The rest was gained as the result of further aggressions by 933 A.D.[39]

The territory thus surrendered by the Frankish king did not cease to form a component part of his empire; the province was only "assigned" to the Normans. In matters of what we now call foreign policy, the Normans associated themselves with the Frankish throne. We can further assume that they substantially adopted the customs of the Franks, including law, faith and language.[40] It is even said that the treaty with Charles the Simple was conditioned upon the Normans adopting Christianity.[41]

Although the history of Normandy was somewhat unclear for the following two or three centuries, there seems to be good reason for accepting Brunner's conclusion that the tradition of the Frankish jury had considerable influence on the courts of William the Conqueror in the following centuries. The widespread use of this type of fact-finding institution required a strong central government. In the remnants of the Frankish empire, strong central authority was maintained only in Flanders and Normandy, while elsewhere the powers of the central government were lost or granted strictly to local strong men.[42] This type of government did not exist in England under the Anglo-Saxons.

As we shall see in chapter four, William the Conqueror made use of the inquisitio almost as soon as the fighting had subsided. Then, as with the Franks, the jury was exercised solely for the benefit of the crown and exclusively at its prerogative. Although certain characteristics of Anglo-Saxon culture were conducive to the reception of a more sophisticated jury system, nothing comparable to the Frankish system was in existence in England at the time of William's invasion. Perhaps the sole exception to this was the isolated instance of an accusing jury. The limited nature of that jury will be noted in chapter three.

Brunner, by comparing language and procedures as contained in documents of the Frankish and Anglo-Norman eras, demonstrated that it was unlikely that the English jury and the Frankish inquisitio had independent origins.[43] The most convincing example offered by Brunner is the suggestion that both Normandy and the Franks gave their respective churches the prerogative to decide land questions by inquisitio, as discussed earlier in this chapter. This was a prerogative that the churches of Normandy were still struggling to maintain throughout the twelfth and thirteenth centuries.[44]

It has been almost exactly one hundred years since Brunner published his work on the origin of the jury. During that time, no scholarship has been able to disprove his conclusions. Pollock and Maitland said, in 1898, that "...but for the conquest of England it [the jury] would have perished..." This work went on to say that this belief overcame the English unwillingness to admit that the "...palladium of our liberties..." was not "...English in origin but Frankish, not popular but royal."[45] Holdsworth said the inquisitio was "...the root from which the English jury springs."[46] Whereas Brunner investigated the earliest origins of the present-day jury, it was James Thayer's intention to continue this discussion through the English tradition.[47] He agreed with many of Brunner's contentions, although W.R. Cornish reasoned that it was more likely that the Normans inherited the jury as an already existing English institution, noting the shift by the Normans to the practice of group inquest after coming in contact with England.[48] However, Dawson, in his work, *A History of Lay Judges*, after weighing the evidence available in 1960, said, "It still seems true, as Brunner contended, that the jury as it entered English law was in all essential respects a royal institution."[49] This is tantamount to saying that the right did not grow up from village assemblies but down from the power of the crown. The inquisitio of Charlemagne may be the father of the jury, but English influence is very apparent. It is to this English preparation that we will now turn.

Chapter II footnotes

1. *A History of Lay Judges*, John P. Dawson (Harvard Univ. Press, 1960), p. 37.

2. "The Origin and Development of Trial By Jury," H.H. Grooms, 26 Ala. Law. 162 (1965).

3. Dawson, *op. cit.* at note 1, at p. 38.

4. *The Origin of Juries*, Heinrich Brunner (Berlin, 1872), p. 98.

5. Dawson, *op. cit.* at note 1, at p. 38.

6. Brunner, *op. cit.* at note 4, at p. 84.

7. Brunner, *op. cit.* at note 4, at pp. 36-37.

8. *The History of English Law*, Sir Frederick Pollock and Frederic William Maitland (2nd Ed., Cambridge Univ. Press, 1898), Vol. I-138.

9. *The Works and Correspondence of Edmund Burke*, Ed. by Charles William and Sir Richard Bourke (London, 1852), Vol. VI-138.

10. Brunner, *op. cit.* at note 4, at p. 87.

11. Brunner, *op. cit.* at note 4, at p. 92.

12. Brunner, *op. cit.* at note 4, at p. 94.

13. Brunner, *op. cit.* at note 4, at p. 95.

14. Brunner, *op. cit.* at note 4, at p. 97.

15. Brunner, *op. cit.* at note 4, at p. 99.

16. Brunner, *op. cit.* at note 4, at p. 101.

17. Brunner, *op. cit.* at note 4, at pp. 104-105.

18. Brunner, *op. cit.* at note 4, at p. 100.

19. Brunner, *op. cit.* at note 4, at pp. 100-01.

20. Brunner, *op. cit.* at note 4, at p. 99.

21. Brunner, *op. cit.* at note 4, at p. 103.

22. Brunner, *op. cit.* at note 4, at pp. 108-10.

23. Brunner, *op. cit.* at note 4, at p. 111.

24. Brunner, *op. cit.* at note 4, at pp. 111-12.

25. Brunner, *op. cit.* at note 4, at p. 111.

26. Brunner, *op. cit.* at note 4, at p. 112.

27. Brunner, *op. cit.* at note 4, at pp. 84-85.

28. *An Enquiry Into the Use and Practice of Juries Among the Greeks and Romans*, John Pettingal (London, 1969), p. 188.

29. Brunner, *op. cit.* at note 4, at pp. 85-86.

30. Brunner, *op. cit.* at note 4, at p. 119.

31. Brunner, *op. cit.* at note 4, at pp. 85-86.

32. *Ibid.*

33. Brunner, *op. cit.* at note 4, at p. 116.

34. Brunner, *op. cit.* at note 4, at p. 103.

35. Brunner, *op. cit.* at note 4, at p. 84.

36. Brunner, *op. cit.* at note 4, at p. 86.

37. Brunner, *op. cit.* at note 4, at p. 114.

38. Brunner, *op. cit.* at note 4, at p. 155.

39. Encyclopedia Britanica (1970), XVI-577.

40. Brunner, *op. cit.* at note 4, at pp. 127-28.

41. Encyclopaedia Britanica, *op. cit.* at note 40 at XVI-577.

42. Dawson, *op. cit.* at note 1, at p. 42.

43. Brunner, *op. cit.* at note 4, at pp. 92 and 118.

44. Brunner, *op. cit.* at note 4, at pp. 96-97.

45. Pollock and Maitland, *op. cit.* at note 8, at I-141.

46. *A History of English Law,* Sir Willian Holdsworth (Sweet and Maxwell, 7th Ed. 1956, 1st Ed. printed in 1903), I-312.

47. *A Preliminary Treatise on Evidence,* James Bradley Thayer (Sweet and Maxwell Ltd., London, 1898), p. 3.

48. *The Jury,* W.R. Cornish (Penguin Press, London, 1962), p. 11.

49. Dawson, *op. cit.* at note 1, at p. 120.

III
The Age of Fire, Water and the Morsel

When the Angles and the Saxons came to Britain, they brought with them Germanic legal procedures which they continued to develop until the Norman conquest. The following description of the Anglo-Saxon system relates principally to the two and one-half centuries before the conquest in 1066 A.D. The legal procedures were not constant from time to time or from place to place, and only rarely did a king of this period exercise authority over more than a single section at a time. It should also be kept in mind that the inhabitants of England at this time were divided into slaves and free men[1]; the legal procedures largely related to the free. Still, the picture of the legal situation that emerges has a strong claim of authenticity.

The judicial system of the Saxons, vertically, had four possible levels of jurisdiction: (1) the tithing (also decenary; i.e., a rural subdivision pertaining to ten); (2) wapentake (pertaining to one hundred); (3) court of the shire or county; and (4) the court of the king or the wittenagemote. This was not necessarily a system whereby appeals were had from the lower to the higher courts, but the king's court could function in that manner. The jurisdiction of the particular court depended on many circumstances, including the importance and notoriety of the case.

Every inhabitant was required to belong to a tithing. The members were responsible for crimes committed by any of their number. In the event a member of the tithing was accused of a crime, the rest were required to arrest him and bring him to justice. If they considered him innocent, they cleared him by their oaths. If he was convicted and sentenced, they had to pay the wergild (man-lot or value, first mentioned in reign of Ethelbert, 568-615 A.D.), essentially the compensation imposed for the crime plus other penalties. If a member of the tithing fled on being accused or suspected of a crime, the members of the tithing had to make an oath that they were not accessories to his flight. Failure to clear themselves again resulted in the members having to pay the wergild.[2] If a stranger sojourned with a family for three days, they were presumed to have made a pledge for him. If a crime took place within the venue of the tithing and it failed to produce the offender within 31 days, the fribourg (head of a tithing) took two principal persons from his own tithing, plus the fribourg and two principal persons from each of the three neighboring tithings. These 12 were to purge the fribourg and his tithing of responsibility for the crime. If the tithing failed by this procedure to clear itself of complicity with the offender or his flight, they had to make compensation to the injured party.[3] On the other hand, if a member of the tithing was injured and received wergild in compensation, the other members of the tithing were entitled to a share.[4]

There were pecuniary values established for injuries, varying according to the time and place committed and the part of the body involved: the ear, 30 shillings; hearing, 60 shillings; front tooth, 8 shillings; canine tooth, 4 shillings; grinding tooth, 16 shillings; a common person bound with chains, 10 shillings; beaten, 20 shillings; or hung up, 30 shillings; damage to an ox's horn, 10 pence; to a cow's horn, 1 pence; fighting in the courtyard of a common person, 6 shillings; or drawn sword only, 3 shillings (if the person who owned the court was worth 600 shillings or more, the amends were tripled and further increases were allowed according to the rank of the person whose premises were violated).[5]

In assessing penalties for other injuries, the starting point was the value set on every man's life, the wergild. In the reign of Aethalstan (924-940 A.D.), these values were as follows: the king, who ranked only as a superior person, 30,000 thrymsae; archbishop or earl, 15,000 thrymsae; bishop, 8,000 thrymsae; priest or thegn, 2,000 thrymsae; common person, 267 thrymsae. The slayer had to make the compensation to the relations of the deceased. If the deceased was a stranger, one-half went to the king and one-half to the companions of the deceased. If the amounts were not paid, the slayer's relations were not required to aid him when feud was instituted against him by the relatives of the deceased. The right of sanctuary in churches was a neces-

sary part of the system because it allowed for time to make ar-
rangements for the payment of the wergild while the feud was
held in abeyance. Those violating sanctuary were punished. According to King Alfred the Great, initiating the feud before
showing a willingness to accept the wergild was punishable.
Also, a person injured by an inanimate object was entitled to
claim it if he acted within 30 days from the time of injury. His
heirs had the right to the object if their relative had been killed,
for example, by a falling tree.[6]

Besides the penalties due the injured party, the guilty person had to pay amounts to the king.[7] For the commission of certain crimes, the guilty person was required to redeem himself by
personal pains; for example, a thief often lost a hand or a foot,
was banished or sold into slavery. Housebreaking, open robbery,
manifest homicide and treason against one's lord were in-
expiable.[8]

Keeping in mind that the above principles were applicable to
all courts, it was the court of the hundred, the wapentake, that
made the biggest impact on the average person of Anglo-Saxon
times.[9] It met once a month and had both civil and criminal jurisdiction. The presiding officer, the elder, was the head man of
the hundreds. He had coordinate authority with the bishop. The
court had cognizance of ecclesiastical matters which were entitled to first preference and which were decided by the
bishop.[10]

The county court met two times a year or more as required.
It was presided over by the shire or reeve, later known as the
sheriff, who was assisted by the bishop. This court had cognizance of causes affecting several hundreds,[11] particularly civil
causes.[12] The real judges of this court were the suitors of the
court (sectatores), who were freemen or landholders who met as
in assembly. The sectatores varied in number; in the time of Aethelred I, (866-871) for example, there were approximately
twelve or more freemen acting in this capacity. They decided
both law and fact, but were not sworn to the truth.[13] One
month after Michaelmas (September 24), the sheriff, accompanied by the bishop, held the most important criminal court of
the year. Also, once a year, during the month after Easter, the

sheriff held the tourn (or circuit). Together with the bishop, he held a view of the frank-pledge; that is, he determined that all persons above the age of 12 years had taken the oath of allegiance, and also found freemen who were pledged to stand responsible for his peaceable demeanor.[14]

The wittenagemote, or king's court, sat with the king, travelling with him whenever necessary. The court was composed of high officers of the state, and it held concurrent jurisdiction with other courts. Generally, its litigation involved causes having to do with the great lords, crimes of a heinous or public nature, and fiscal affairs of the state.[15] This court also served as a court of appeal from the county court and the other courts of a more limited nature.[16]

The system of law and police regulation as described in this chapter was more or less complete at the time of King Alfred the Great (871-899 A.D.).[17] Apparently, King Alfred took the quality of justice rendered in his courts quite seriously. The *Mirror of Justices*, written no later than 1290 A.D., relates that the king ordered no fewer than 44 of his justices to be hanged as murderers in one year for false judgments. One judge was hanged because he gave the death sentence as a result of testimony by 12 men who had not been sworn. Another judge met his fate because his jurors* were in doubt of their verdict and in "...doubtful causes one ought rather to save than to condemn."[18]

Before the conquest of England, a charge or claim had to be supported by an oath (after the conquest, it had to be supported by witnesses or the secta.)[19] The coroner's office existed before the conquest, this being mentioned in connection with a matter concerning the Monastery of Beverly in 925 A.D. during the reign of Aethelstan (924 - 940 A.D.).[20] The system of canon law was well developed by 1100 A.D., and although it was no doubt much advanced by the time of the conquest, it was not established as a separate court until the time of the conquest. The written procedure for canon law ordinarily commenced with a

---

* [The reference to "jurors" above was not intended in the modern sense, but rather refers to a type of sectatore or compurgator in the various kinds of witness proof that will be mentioned hereafter.]

statement of claim, followed by a counterclaim. Interrogatories were drawn up by the parties in preparation for questioning by the judge of witnesses, and lastly, the judge's written record of his findings and judgments was included. The witnesses were sworn.[21]

The English claim to have originated the jury is founded on the legislation of such rulers as Aethelred I (865-871 A.D.), Alfred the Great (871-899) and Aethelred II, the Unready (978-1013). Good examples of this legislation were the statutes of Aethelred I:[22]

> Let doom stand where thanes are of one voice: if they disagree, let that stand which seven of them say; and let those who are there out voted pay each of them six half marks.

This statute relates to Wales:

> Twelve laymen shall administer the law (or explain it) to the British and English; six English and six British. Let them forfeit all they possess if they administer it wrongly, or let them clear themselves that they know no better.

King Alfred issued this statute:

> If a royal thane be accused of homicide he shall purge himself with twelve royal thanes. Any other man shall purge himself with eleven of his own rank and one royal thane.[23]

Aethelred II issued a law which affected only the Danish district of England. In essence it declared that a moot would be held in every wapentake in which the twelve oldest thegns would go out with the reeve and swear upon the relic that he would put into their hands that they would accuse no innocent person and conceal no guilty man.[24]

The courts instituted by the two Aethelreds are best understood as accusing bodies. They differed from grand juries in that the appointments were more or less permanent and the members served more as lay assessors than as jurors.[25] The law of Alfred clearly relates to compurgators.[26] Generally, the statutes creating these accusing courts fell into disuse, and thereafter accusations were usually made by the voice of the community; i.e., at the assemblies held in connection with the local courts.[27]

There is yet one more example of something similar to a jury trial before 1066 A.D. During the reign of Edward the Confessor (1024-1066 A.D.), the parties to a boundary dispute voluntarily submitted the settlement of the matter to a group of neighbors who were sworn.[28] This comes as close to the civil jury as we are likely to find in England before the conquest, but it does not appear to be the result of any general statute, and does not necessarily seem, on the basis of the information available, to have been summoned by royal authority. When we examine the jury after the conquest we will find that it was invariably summoned by a royal writ.

The various courts that we have been examining were generally accusing bodies as far as criminal matters were concerned (except when charges were brought by individuals). In both civil and criminal matters, although both were occasionally decided by the voice of the assemblies, the courts generally directed the mode of proof that would finally determine the litigation. Four different modes of proof were: (1) proof by oath; (2) by official witnesses; (3) by compurgation; and (4) by ordeal.

The trial by oath, apparently used in less serious matters, might be resorted to after a defendant's testimony was challenged or contradicted by the plaintiff or accuser. The defendant was required to repeat his denial under oath according to an exact formula. Oath came to be piled upon oath, the slightest deviation resulting in the defendant losing his case. This became so risky that many avoided this type of trial by choosing the judgment of God — that is, the ordeal.[29]

Official witness proof first appeared in Anglo-Saxon law in 924 A.D. during the first year of Aethelstan. Witnesses were appointed to attest to bargains, much as notaries did in later English history. (This was perhaps the origin of that institution as far as England is concerned.)[30] King Eadgar the Peaceful (959-975) decreed that thirty witnesses for each town, or twelve witnesses for small towns and every hundred, should be appointed to swear to make true depositions. From their number, two or three were brought to witness all commercial transactions. When there was a dispute, the party attempting to prove the transaction had to produce these persons as witnesses. The testimony of commercial witnesses was conclusive.[31] This law is also suggested to be another possible precursor of the modern jury by reason of the mention of the number 12. It is said that this type of proof died out after the conquest,[32] but it is probably an ancestor of the deed witness.

In trial by compurgation, as in other Anglo-Saxon actions, the matter was initiated by the fore-oath of the person bringing the action. The defendant would prove his innocence by taking this oath: "By the Lord, I am guiltless both in deed and counsel of the charge of which N. accuses me."

His compurgators would support him with this oath: "By the Lord, the oath is clear and unperjured which M. has sworn."

The value of the oath of the compurgators varied according to the defendant's rank, as measured by the wergild or by the hydes of land he possessed (a hyde was equal to 33 acres). A person of bad character might be required to obtain three times the ordinary number of compurgators or undergo the ordeal. A person caught in the very act of his crime could not clear himself by compurgation. In such an instance, the ordeal was necessary, if a trial was held at all.[33] Compurgation in regular cases, however, if successful, was a complete acquittal.[34] For the mildest crimes, three compurgators sufficed; for more severe matters, six were required; to the most atrocious charges, the defendant had to produce 11 compurgators, with his own oath making the twelfth. Unanimity was naturally required of these witnesses inasmuch as the compurgators were all chosen by the defendant himself.[35]

More popular as a mode of trial was the judgment of God, called the ordeal. It is said that this method of finding truth was given by God to Moses around the year 1450 B.C. The detailed account of the founding of this institution is recorded in the Bible, in Numbers, chapter five, verses 12 to 31. Moses was told that a man who suspected his wife of being unfaithful, but having no proof, should bring her to the priest together with an

ephah of barley meal (a little over a bushel) with no oil or frank-
incense on it. The priest was to set the woman before the Lord,
take clean water in an earthen vessel and add to it dust from the
tabernacle floor. He would then uncover the woman's head and
place the grain offering in her hands. The priest would hold
"...the water of contention that brings out the truth..." and put
the woman under oath. The priest would then say to the
woman:

> If no man has had intercourse with you, if you have
> not gone astray and let yourself become defiled while
> owing obedience to your husband, then may your in-
> nocence be established by the water of contention
> which brings out the truth. But if, while owing him
> obedience, you have gone astray and let yourself be-
> come defiled, if any man other than your husband has
> had intercourse with you (the priest shall here put the
> woman under oath with an adjuration, and shall con-
> tinue), may the Lord make an example of you among
> your people in adjurations and in swearing oaths by
> bringing upon you miscarriage and untimely birth; and
> this water that brings out the truth shall enter your
> body, bringing upon you miscarriage and untimely
> birth.[36]

The woman answered, "Amen, amen," and the priest wrote
the curse on a scroll and washed the scrolls in the water of contention, making the woman drink the water. The priest then
took the grain offering for jealousy from the woman and
presented it as a gift before the Lord at the altar. A handful of
grain was taken and burned at the altar, and the woman again
drank of the water of contention.[37]

Charlemagne is sometimes credited with having instituted
the ordeal with the words, "Let doubtful cases be determined by
the judgment of God."[38] However, the ordeal is more popularly
attributed to Bishop Poppo. It is recorded that he preached to
the Jutlanders of Denmark, having little success. The bishop
asked them if they would believe that the message he preached
was divine if he could touch hot iron and suffer no harm. Having obtained agreement to this, he had prepared an iron glove

which was heated until it was red hot. He thrust his hand into the glove, withdrew it uninjured and the Northmen were suitably impressed.[39]

However, it would seem that the ordeal was present in England before this time. We do know without question that the ordeal was common in England before the conquest, principally in the forms of fire and water. Ordeal would be required when a party had insufficient compurgators, when he had previously been guilty of perjury, or if he was not a freeman. Of course, the accused had to swear to his innocence before undergoing the ordeal.[40]

In one form of ordeal by fire, hot iron of a pound weight had to be carried nine feet. The hand was then wrapped and sealed. On the third day the accused came to the altar and the hand was unwrapped. If it was not in some way festered or infected, he was innocent, otherwise he was guilty.[41] In a variation, the accused would walk blindfolded and barefooted over nine red-hot plowshares.[42] In addition, the ordeal could be simple, double or triple, known as the threefold judgment of God. In the double ordeal, the weight of the iron was increased to two pounds and, in the triple, to three pounds. Whether the ordeal was to be simple, double or triple depended upon the trustworthiness of the accused as determined by the accusing thegns.[43]

Ordeal by water was either hot or cold. In the hot water version, the hand was put into boiling water up to the wrist, elbow or shoulder, depending on whether the ordeal was simple, double or triple. A variation of this was the requirement that the accused pick a stone out of the boiling water. After that, the same procedure was followed as in the ordeal of hot iron. If the accused was adjudged to undergo the cold water ordeal, he was bound thumb to toes and thrown into water. If he sank, he was innocent. If he floated, the water was considered to have rejected him, and he was guilty.[44] Of course, if he sank, he was retrieved.

These were not the only types of ordeal. One ordeal that was popular among priests, perhaps because it was the safest, was the ordeal of the accused morsel, sometimes a piece of con-secrated bread of the Eucharist. The accused would say a prayer asking that he choke while swallowing the bread if he had not sworn the truth concerning his guilt. Godwine, Earl of Kent and Wessex, is supposed to have died in the attempt of this ordeal in 1053 A.D.[45] If the ordeal of the cross was selected as the mode of trial, the accused was blindfolded and given the choice of two sticks. One had a cross carved on it. If he chose that one, he was innocent.[46]

The ordeal was essentially a religious ceremony. Three days before the trial, the accused sought help from the priest, was constantly at mass, made offerings, and lived only on bread, wa-ter and onions. On the day of the trial he received Communion, and both he and the accuser came to the place of the trial in the company of not more than 12 persons each. If the accused ap-peared with more than 12, he was convicted automatically. At the time and place appointed, both the accuser and the accused renewed under oath, respectively, the charge and denial. The ac-cused then proceeded to the ordeal which had been adjudged, as described above. The priest was present during the entire cere-mony for the necessary religious rituals; for example, before the ordeal of hot iron, the priest would sprinkle the hot iron with holy water.[47] After 1066 A.D., these modes of trial continued, some lasting for centuries in varying degrees, while others died out. This, then, was the state of Anglo-Saxon law as it existed prior to the time of the Norman conquest.

Chapter III Footnotes

1. *History of the English Law*, John Reeves (Reed and Hunter, London, 1814), I-5.

2. *History of Trial by Jury*, William Forsyth (John Parker and Son, London, 1852), pp. 56-57, 60-61.

3. Reeves, *op. cit.* at note 1, at I-13.

4. Forsyth, *op. cit.* at note 2, at p. 61.

5. Reeves, *op. cit.* at note 1, at I-13.

6. Reeves, *op. cit.* at note 1, at I-15-17, 19.

7. Forsyth, *op. cit.* at note 2, at p. 59.

8. Reeves, *op. cit.* at note 1, at I-16.

9. *A History of Lay Judges,* John P. Dawson (Harvard Univ. Press, 1960), p. 182.

10. Forsyth, *op. cit.* at note 2, at p. 63.

11. *Ibid.*

12. Reeves, *op. cit.* at note 1, at I-7.

13. Reeves, *op. cit.* at note 1, at I-22-23; *The Origin of Juries,* Heinrich Brunner (Berlin, 1872), p. 400.

14. Reeves, *op. cit.* at note 1, at I-6-7.

15. Reeves, *op. cit.* at note 1, at I-7-8.

16. Forsyth, *op. cit.* at note 2, at p. 64.

17. Reeves, *op. cit.* at note 1, at I-13.

18. *The Mirror of Justices,* Andrew Horn, translated from the French by William Hughes in 1646, original written about 1285-90 (His Majesty's Law Printers, London, 1768), pp. 239-40.

19. Brunner, *op. cit.* at note 13, at pp. 428-29.

20. Forsyth, *op. cit.* at note 2, at p. 225.

21. Dawson, *op. cit.* at note 9, at p. 45.

22. Forsyth, *op. cit.* at note 2, at p. 67.

23. Brunner, *op. cit.* at note 13, at p. 402.

24. *The History of English Law,* Sir Frederick Pollock and Frederic William Maitland (Cambridge Univ. Press, 1898), I-142-43.

25. Reeves, *op. cit.* at note 1, at p. 23.

26. *Ibid.*

27. Forsyth, *op. cit.* at note 2, at p. 194.

28. Dawson, *op. cit.* at note 9, at p. 120.

29. Brunner, *op. cit.* at note 13, at p. 398; *A Preliminary Treatise on Evidence,* James Bradley Thayer (Sweet and Maxwell Ltd., London, 1898), p. 24.

30. Forsyth, *op. cit.* at note 2, at p. 84.

31. Forsyth, *op. cit.* at note 2, at p. 89.

32. Brunner, *op. cit.* at note 13, at p. 399.

33. Forsyth, *op. cit.* at note 2, at pp. 73-79.

34. Reeves, *op. cit.* at note 1, at I-20.

35. *Trial by Jury,* Thorl. Gudn. Repp (Thomas Clark, 1832), pp. 38-39.

36. *The New English Bible* (Oxford Univ. Press and Cambridge Univ. Press, 1970), Numbers V-19-23.

37. "Origin and Development of Trial by Jury," Robert H. White, 29 Tenn. L. Rev. 8, 9 (1961-62).

38. *Ibid.*

39. Forsyth, *op. cit.* at note 2, at p. 17.

40. Forsyth, *op. cit.* at note 2, at pp. 63, 80.

41. "Early Opposition to the Petty Jury In Criminal Cases," Charles L. Wells, 30 Law. Q. Rev. 97, at 98 (1914).

42. "The Origin and Development of Trial by Jury," H.H. Grooms, 26 Ala. Law. 162, at 163 (1965).

43. Brunner, *op. cit.* at note 13, at p. 404.

44. Forsyth, *op. cit.* at note 2, at pp. 80-81; Brunner, *Ibid;* Wells, *op. cit.* at note 41 at p. 98; Reeves, *op. cit.* at note 1, at I-20.

45. Forsyth, *Ibid.;* Wells, *Ibid.;* Reeves, *op. cit.* at note 1, at I-21-22.

46. Reeves, *op. cit.* at note 1, at I-22.

47. Reeves, *op. cit.* at note 1, at I-21.

IV

William the Conqueror—
Henry the Administrator,
1066-1205 A.D.

Harold's defeat by William the Conqueror at the Battle of Hastings (1066)[1] was highly significant in terms of the long-range consequences for British culture and law, although even in the short run changes were quickly apparent. In 1070, an inquest into the laws of England was conducted by William, as he intended to rule the English by these already existing laws.[2]

He also began a vast series of inquests in every county of England, which were possibly begun as early as 1083, and which were completed in the year 1086. The king's justices summoned a jury in every county consisting of the sheriff, the bailiff of each manor, the reeve of each hundred, the priest and some villeins. This jury was required to determine under oath the value and manner of holding of all property within the county in the time of Edward the Confessor, at the time it came into the present holder's hands, and at the time of the inquest.[3] The result of these surveys was known as the Domesday Books, the extensive records of population and landholdings throughout England.

An instance of something closer to a modern trial jury was the inquest summoned to determine what lands were held by the church at Ely on the day of the Confessor's death. A dispute had arisen when a sheriff had treated certain lands as belonging to the king which were also claimed by the Bishop of Rochester. The moots of several shires from the neighborhood were summoned to decide the dispute, with the Bishop of Bayeaux presiding over it. The jurors, fearing the king, found in his favor. The bishop wasn't satisfied with the verdict and thus directed the jurors to retire and select 12 of their number who would

35

confirm the verdict under oath. They returned the same verdict, but recanted when a monk gave new testimony and they were subsequently questioned individually by the bishop. The land, or at least that part of it which was not claimed by a specific order of the Conqueror, was restored to the church.[4]

King William was the first to generally appoint professional justices. He separated the ecclesiastical courts from the secular courts and introduced the duel.[5] He replaced the foreoath with plaint witnesses. An unsupported claim had been insufficient under both Norman and Anglo-Saxon law to require a defendant to call a witness or produce proof. The Anglo-Saxon claimant supported his cause with an oath, the Norman with a plaint witness. The number of plaint witnesses required by William were two. These witnesses, called the secta, were persons who supported the plaintiff's claim in advance of an answer by the defendant. The secta were not sworn, but the judge would examine them, both for purposes of identification and to make certain that they were in agreement with the claim of the plaintiff. The burden of proof remained with the defendant. The use of the secta faded out in the thirteenth and fourteenth centuries.[6] In fact, although it had been the intention to keep Anglo-Saxon law in practice, Norman law nonetheless made a deep impression on English society.

Henry I reigned from 1100 to 1132, during which time there are recorded at least two inquests by juries. The first took place on the order of Henry's son, William, sometime prior to 1120. The writ was directed to the sheriff of Kent who was ordered to summon an inquest to resolve a conflict between the Abbey of St. Augustine and the king's treasury, concerning the rights to a vessel which had been taken. A second writ ordered the vessel restored to the abbey on the basis of the results of the inquest.[7]

In 1121, Henry I commanded that a dispute between the monastery of St. Stephen and the Exchequer be decided by an inquest of neighbors. Sixteen men served on this inquest, although attempts to avoid jury duty were still prevalent.[8] It should be noted that an individual mandate was required for each case, as was true in the time of the Franks.[9]

Henry II ruled England from 1154 until 1189, introducing more far reaching legal changes than any other monarch that ever held that throne. If a single person could be thought of as creating the jury, he would be that person. The first of a series of great enactments which have come down to us from this period was the Constitution of Clarendon (1164). One provision was directed at powerful individuals who were attempting to intimidate others in order to escape prosecution. It provided, "...The sheriff shall cause 12 legal men of the neighborhood, or of the fill, to take an oath in the presence of the bishop that they will declare the truth about it."[10] This jury was also empowered to declare a verdict of guilt or innocence, thus going beyond the duty of older accusatory courts.[11] Another provision provided for an inquest (jury) to decide whether land was subject to the jurisdiction of the king's court or was church property and therefore subject to the ecclesiastical courts. Apparently the language of this statute indicated that the custom of holding an inquest on this subject was ancient; the churches of the Franks and the Normans also struggled for a similar right.[12] These passages contain the first suggestion of something similar to the modern jury that has come down to us in the English statutes,[13] although the text has not survived completely intact.[14]

Of all the legislation of Henry II, the Grand Assize (Assize of Clarendon, 1066 A.D.) was to prove the most far reaching in terms of establishing the jury. It is set forth most clearly in *A Treatise on the Laws and Customs of the Kingdom of England*, by Ranulph de Glanville.[15] Whether Glanville actually wrote the treatise is immaterial; what is significant is that the work was written in 1181 and is the earliest treatise that has come down to us on English law. Glanville was the chief justiciar of England under Henry II from 1180 until the king's death in 1189, and thus it might be interesting to note the high points in the career of this man who came to be King Henry II's chief judge and executor of his will.

Glanville was sheriff of Yorkshire from 1163 until the Sheriff's Inquest in 1170, when Henry II removed all sheriffs and instituted an inquiry into their administrations. Glanville supported the king during the great rebellion of 1173, and as a result was made sheriff of Lancashire. Glanville and two other leaders won a great victory over the Scots on July 13, 1174. He was made judge in 1176, the Count of Flanders in 1177, and Chief Justiciar ("the king's eye") of all England in 1180. In 1182 he again took to the field leading an army against the Welsh. He was also present at the coronation of Richard I (the Lionhearted) in September, 1189, and accompanied King Richard on a crusade to the Holy Land in 1190. Although Glanville was rather old for campaigning, Richard had no desire to leave such an influential individual behind in England during an extended absence. Glanville died at the siege of Acon in 1190 either "fighting valiantly," according to one report, or according to another, as a result of the eastern climate.[16]

The Grand Assize, as described by Glanville, was a court designed by Henry II. It was intended to give a person whose possession of land was challenged (the tenant) the alternative to put himself on the Grand Assize (an inquest of four knights and 12 neighbors) or to decide the issue with a duel. When the tenant elected the Grand Assize, the demandant (claimant to the land) was bound to consent to it unless there was a special reason why the Assize was not appropriate; for example, if the parties were descended from a common ancestor from whom they both claimed title.

If the matter of the relationship was disputed, the relatives of both parties were consulted. The question would be settled if the relations were in agreement; if not, the question was referred to the vincinage, or neighborhood, whose decision was final. If no relationship was shown, the demandant lost his case for wrongfully attempting to deprive the tenant of his right to the Grand Assize. If the matter of relationship was confirmed, the Assize was completed and the verdict wad determined verbally by the court as a matter of law as to which of the two parties was the rightful heir.

It was necessary for the tenant to get two other writs while the Grand Assize was in progress. The first required the demandant to keep the peace, and the second prohibited other courts from proceeding with the action otherwise. At this point, the demandant would cause the following writ to issue:

The King to the Sheriff, Health.

Summon by good summoners, four lawful Knights of the Vincinage of Stoke, that they be at the Pentecost before me, or my Justices, at Westminster, to elect on their oaths, twelve lawful Knights of that Vincinage, who better know the truth, to return, on their oaths, whether M. or R. have the greater right in one Hyde of land in Stoke, which M. claims against R. by my Writ, and of which R. the Tenant hath put himself upon my Assize and prays a Recognition [inquest] to be made, which of them have the greater right in that land. . . .

At the time set, the knights appeared and elected the jurors. Both parties had a right to be present at the election and challenge for good cause members of the proposed jury. If the tenant did not appear, the selection of the jury was not interrupted, but it did not continue if the demandant failed to appear. After the election of the 12, they were summoned ". . .to appear in court, prepared upon their oaths to declare, which of them, namely, whether the tenant, or the demandant, possess the greater right to the property in question."

A key word in understanding the role played by the jurors at the trial was "prepared." It was usual for the jurors to inform themselves about the dispute before appearing in court. The writ also provided for the jurors to view the land before coming to court. If it developed that the jurors testified under oath that they were unacquainted with the facts, other jurors were summoned until there were 12 who had knowledge and who agreed. Knowledge did not mean first-hand knowledge, but declarations of a juror's father or other equally reliable sources were sufficient. The jurors of this court were knights, and their decision was conclusive of the dispute.

Glanville referred to the Grand Assize as a ". . . certain royal benefit bestowed upon the people, and emanating from the clemency of the Prince. . . ." He listed the following as among its benefits: (1) The owner possessed his right to the land in safety pending the outcome of litigation; (2) It avoided the uncertain outcome of the duel; (3) It avoided unexpected and premature death; (4) It avoided the "... opprobrium of a lasting infamy, of that dreadful and ignominious word [craven] that so disgracefully resounds from the mouth of the conquered champion;" (5) It was less expensive and more efficient; and (6) The verdict was necessarily more just than the result of a duel.[17]

The Assize of Clarendon of 1166 also provided that those accused by the public inquest (grand jury), as established by the Constitution of Clarendon (1164), should be tried by ordeal. This eliminated trial by compurgation and duel in a great many cases.[18] A statute of 1176, however, provided that if one accused of murder or a felony passed the ordeal, he would nonetheless be banished.[19] The term "Assize of Novel Disseisin" is often used synonymously with the Grand Assize, but it would seem that Novel Disseisin ought to be reserved for those causes in which there was a claim that the dispossession was recent. For example, note the writ to the sheriff under Novel Disseisin from Glanville:

> ...summon by good summoners, twelve free and lawful men of the neighborhood of such a Vill, ... prepared on their oath to return, if T., the father of the aforesaid G., was seised in his Demesne as of fee, of one yardland, in that Vill, on the day of his death — if he died after my first coronation [Oct. 20, 1154], and if said G. be his nearer heir, and, in the meantime, let them view the land and cause their names to be imbreviated....[20]

Another example of recent dispossession under the jurisdiction of Novel Disseisin was when the dispossession had occurred after a voyage of the king into Normandy.[21]

This is only a sample of the various uses of neighborhood inquests during the reign of Henry II. Aside from those mentioned, there was the Assize of Northampton in 1176 (including the Assize of Uttrum and the Assize Mort d' Ancestor);[22] the Assize of Darrein presentment at the Council at Windsor, 1179;[23] the Assize of Arms, 1181;[24] and the Assize of the Forest, 1184.[25] However, this list does not exhaust the use of the inquest during the reign of Henry II. Clearly the jury was by this time a substantial legal remedy.

All the above uses of the jury were held by reason of a royal writ. Along with the development of these formal procedures,[26] there developed trials where the parties, by their own consent, submitted for arbitration some question of fact to an inquest of their neighbors. This form of the jury was called the jurata. The jurors of this court were not sworn with regard to a particular dispute, and had no chance to gather facts about the dispute before being sworn. The view of the scene, if had, was held after the taking of the oath. Since the parties had consented to the tribunal, the jurors could not be attacked by attaint; that is, for rendering a false verdict.[27] It was felt that since the jurors had not had a chance to inform themselves of the situation prior to the trial, it would not be fair to punish them if their verdict miscarried.[28] This form of tribunal, however, was used only for a short time.[29]

The trial jury in criminal cases was brought into use after the civil jury.[30] The criminal jury was present in England in the time of Glanville (i.e., before 1190) but it was little used.[31]

There has been much speculation as to why juries consist of 12 members. Devlin plausibly suggests that this was the number most traditionally used in the wager of law or compurgation.[32] Through the reign of King John, however, 12 was not invariably the number; e.q., Brunner found the numbers of jurors ranging from 6 to 66. Specific examples are given of juries of six existing in a part of Cornwall and also in Wales during the reign of Henry VIII.[33] Thayer found a jury of nine in 1199, and juries of 9, 36 and 40 between the years 1217-1219.[34]

Curious speculation on the origin of the use of 12 members for a jury is contained in a 1682 guide to juries:

> It seems as if very anciently the number on a jury was indefinite, but it was all the persons present, come as would come.... But in analogy of late it's reduced to the number of twelve, like as the Prophets were twelve, to foretell the Truth; the Apostles twelve, to Preach the Truth; the Discoverers twelve, sent into Canan to see and report the Truth; and the Stones twelve, that the Heavenly Hieruslaem is built on: And

as the Judges were twelve anciently to try and determine matters of Law.

And always when there is any waging Law, there
must be twelve to swear in it; and also as for matters
of State, there were formerly twelve councellors of
State. And any thing now which any Jury can be said
to do, must have the joynt consent of twelve.... Else
it's in construction of Law, not the doing of the Jury,
but of Private Persons, and void.[35]

The basic qualifications of jurors involved being free and a
property owner, although the statutory inquests mentioned
above required that the jurors be knights. As has also been
noted, the jurors were witnesses summoned from the neighborhood.[36] As the duel fell into disuse, the official witnesses came
to be included on the jury panel.[37]

The jury at this point seldom held the power to actually decide questions of law,[38] although jurors did not have to rely
solely on evidence presented in court; e.g., in a case in 1200, the
members of a jury rejected a deed given in evidence, ruling contrary to it and relying on their own knowledge.[39] Jurors could be
objected to for a previous conviction of perjury, serfdom, con-
sanguinity, affinity, enmity or close friendship. There could be
an objection to the entire array if it had not been selected by a
disinterested person. In early times, it was even permitted to
challenge the judge, although this right was soon lost. Eventually, the jury of the Grand Assize was sworn by having one
member take the oath, while the others promised to uphold it as
it applied to them.[40]

The principle of unanimity was not firmly established before the thirteenth century, although in the Grand Assize, 12 of
16 had to agree.[41] The knights on the early juries could render a
special verdict if they chose not to render a general verdict, and
leave it to the judges to apply the law to those facts. In fact, one
of the reasons for using the jury during the reign of Henry II
was that it saved the time of trained judges.[42]

As the jurors were considered to have personal knowledge
of the truth of the matter in dispute and were not, like modern

jurors, responsible for judging the credibility of witnesses who presented conflicting testimony, they were held guilty of perjury for rendering a false verdict.[43] The first notice of the punishment rendered for a false verdict in the legal literature of England is found in Glanville. He said those jurors who confessed to or were convicted of perjury would lose all their "chattles" (moveable property) which were forfeited to the king, "although by the great clemency of the Prince; their freehold tenements are spared. They shall also be thrown into prison and there detained for one year at least." They were also held incompetent as witnesses.[44]

The procedure of punishing jurors for false verdicts was called attaint. The issue is tried by another jury, usually consisting of 24 members, who heard only the evidence presented to the first jury. If the first jury had heard other testimony they might have reached a different result. There was no attaint in criminal matters,[45] and, in the fiscal affairs of the king, attaint was only used if the verdict was against the king.[46] The attaint was not used in the Grand Assize because it replaced the duel which, by its nature, allowed no appeal.[47]

The jury appeared in Scotland during the reign of King David (1124-1153) and spread outward from his court in much the same manner as in England.[48] Coroners were making use of juries for inquests from at least the early thirteenth century.[49] The Court of Common Pleas was taking distinct form by the late twelfth century.[50] Along with the jury, William the Conqueror had brought the trappings of feudalism to England, which included courts of lords responsible for deciding causes between the lords and vassals.[51] The sheriff became a crown agent and held hearings in the shire courts, but his power gradually declined.[52] As has been noted above, the ecclesiastical courts were separated from the secular courts by the year 1100.[53] These courts dealt with matters of status such as birth, death, marriage and bastardy. They also heard causes where it was alleged that oral contract had been broken, on the theory that it was a question of broken faith.[54]

Compurgation continued to play a limited role after the conquest, but it was replaced to a large extent by the duel which was the ordinary mode of proof in the twelfth century until the Constitution of Clarendon.[55] The duel was not suitable for some parties; e.g., women, minors, relatives, the blind, deaf, or a person who had become incompetent to be a witness by reason of having been convicted of perjury.[56] The duel was restricted as early as Henry I (1100-1135) in cases where the property in question was of small value.[57] The assizes of Henry II did not eliminate trials by combat but only restricted the occasions for their use.[58]

Andrew Horne, the author of *The Mirror of Justices*[59], attributed the origin of trial by battle to the biblical David and Goliath. Noting that no one may substitute for another in combat, he proceeded to describe the duel. At the place of trial, the priest first delivered a benediction and then a malediction. The defendant then swore that he was not guilty, and the accuser swore that the defendant was a perjurer. The combatants had their heads, arms and hands uncovered, but their legs and feet were armed with iron, and they carried a shield of iron. Their weapons may have been staves.[60] The accuser was the first to "come into the list," entering from the east. The defendant entered from the west, and they both swore that they had not eaten or drunk anything whereby the truth might be "disturbed and the devil enhanced."

A judge would then make a proclamation warning, under threat of punishment, against the disturbance of the combat by observers. Then the combatants came together. They fought until one was killed, uttered the word craven, uncovered his left foot, or until the sun went down. If there was no decision by the time the sun set, the defendant had judgment. According to Glanville, "champions" were permitted, although they could not be paid,[61] and if the duel was lost by a champion or by the party in person, there was a fine imposed in addition to the suit being lost. The defeated champion was not permitted to appear as a witness thereafter in court. In the Grand Assize, there was an exception to the rule that a party was allowed to appear in person. The demandant could not appear in his own person because of the need of a witness who had seen and heard the fact. The tenant, however, could appear in person as well as by a champion.[62]

This was the world of the jury into the early thirteenth century and before the Magna Carta. In 1205 Phillip Augustus, King of France, invaded Normandy and, finding little resistance, conquered the province.[63] The result was that the jury died in Normandy, while continuing in England. From this point forward it therefore is proper to speak of the English jury, as opposed to the Anglo-Norman jury.

Chapter IV Footnotes

1. *A History of Lay Judges,* John P. Dawson (Harvard Univ. Press, Cambridge, Mass., 1960), pp. 116-17.

2. *The Englishman's Right,* Sir John Hawles (first printed 1680, 6th Ed. in London, 1771), p. 5.

3. *Domesday Book Relating to Essex,* translated from the Latin by T.C. Chisenhall-Marsh (London, 1864), p. 2.

4. *History of the English Law,* John Reeves (Reed and Hunter, London, 1814), I-84; *History of Trial By Jury,* William Forsyth (John Parker and Son, London, 1852), pp. 100-03; *The History of English Law,* Sir Frederick Pollock and Frederic William Maitland (Cambridge Univ. Press, 1898) I-143. The version in each of these three authorities varies, but they have reference to the same incident.

5. Forsyth, *op. cit.* at note 4, at pp. 96-98.

6. *The Origin of Juries,* Heinrich Brunner (Berlin, 1872), p. 430, and *A Preliminary Treatise on Evidence,* James Bradley Thayer (Sweet and Maxwell, London, 1898), p. 13.

7. *Id.* at p. 219.

8. Brunner, *op. cit.* at note 6, pp. 354-55.

9. Brunner, *op. cit.* at note 6, pp. 218-19.

10. "The Origin of the Petty Jury," Charles L. Wells, 27 Law Q. Rev. 347 (1911).

11. Forsyth, *op. cit.* at note 4, at p. 195.

12. Pollock and Maitland, *op. cit.* at note 4, at I-145.

13. Forsyth, *op. cit.* at note 4, at p. 136.

14. Brunner, *op. cit.* at note 6, at p. 300.

15. *A Translation of Glanville,* John Beames, Esq. (London, 1812).

16. *Id.* at pp. xiii-xviii of the preface; *Dictionary of National Biography* (London, 1890), Vol. XXI-413-14.

17. Beames, *op. cit.* at note 15, pp. 37-66.

18. "Early Opposition to the Petty Jury In Criminal Cases," Charles Wells, 30 Law Q. Rev. 97, at 98 (1914); *Trial By Jury,* Sir Patrick Devlin (Stevens and Sons Ltd., London, 1966), pp. 8-9.

19. Wells, *op. cit.* at note 18, at p. 98.

20. Beames, *op. cit.* at note 15, at p. 306.

21. Beames, *op. cit.* at note 15, at p. 335.

22. Forsyth, *op. cit.* at note 4, at p. 136.

23. Pollock and Maitland, *op. cit.* at note 4, at I-148.

24. Thayer, *op. cit.* at note 6, at p. 57.

25. *Ibid.*

26. Forsyth, *op. cit.* at note 4, at pp. 135, 143; Brunner, *op. cit.* at note 6, at p. 260.

27. Brunner, *op. cit.* at note 6, at pp. 416-17.

28. Brunner, *op. cit.* at note 6, at pp. 421, 423.

29. Brunner, *op. cit.* at note 6, at pp. 421-22.

30. Brunner, *op. cit.* at note 6, at pp. 42-43.

31. Forsyth, *op. cit.* at note 4, at pp. 64-65.

32. Devlin, *op. cit.* at note 18, at p. 48.

33. Brunner, *op. cit.* at note 6, at pp. 273-4, 364.

34. Thayer, *op. cit.* at note 6, at p. 86.

35. *A Guide to English Juries,* by a Person of Quality (Forsyth attributed this work to Lord Somers) (London, 1682), pp. 9-11.

36. Devlin, *op. cit.* at note 18, at p. 17.

37. Forsyth, *op. cit.* at note 4, at p. 151.

38. Brunner, *op. cit.* at note 6, at p. 286.

39. Thayer, *op. cit.* at note 6, at pp. 90-1, 105.

40. Forsyth, *op. cit.* at note 4, at pp. 137, 176-77.

41. Brunner, *op. cit.* at note 6, at pp. 366, 369.

42. Dawson, *op. cit.* at note 1, at p. 293.

43. Devlin, *op. cit.* at note 18, at p. 67.

44. Beames, *op. cit.* at note 15, at pp. 67-68.

45. Devlin, *op. cit.* at note 18, at pp. 67-68.

46. Brunner, *op. cit.* at note 6, at p. 424.

47. Thayer, *op. cit.* at note 6, at p. 156.

48. Pollock and Maitland, *op. cit.* at note 4, at I-144.

49. Pollock and Maitland, *op. cit.* at note 4, at II-643.

50. Dawson, *op. cit.* at note 1, at p. 56.

51. Dawson, *op. cit.* at note 1, at p. 118.

52. *Ibid.*

53. Forsyth, *op. cit.* at note 4, at p. 96.

54. Beames, *op. cit.* at note 15, at p. 180; Forsyth, *op. cit.* at note 4, at p. 151.

55. Brunner, *op. cit.* at note 6, at p. 181.

56. Brunner, *op. cit.* at note 6, at pp. 182-83.

57. Beames, *op. cit.* at note 15, a footnote on pp. 40-41.

58. Brunner, *op. cit.* at note 6, at pp. 251, 348-49.

59. *The Mirror of Justices*, Andrew Horne, translated by William Hughes, 1646 (London, 1768), at p. 157-62.

60. Beames, *op. cit.* at note 15, at a footnote on pp. 40-41.

61. Beames, *op. cit.* at note 14, at p. 46.

62. *Ibid.*

63. Brunner, *op. cit.* at note 6, at p. 136.

V
Evolution of the Judgment Jury: 1205-1400

In the law of English speaking people, the Magna Carta has loomed large since it was issued by King John on June 15, 1215. This charter has commonly been credited with guaranteeing trial by jury. Blackstone wrote in the 1760's that:

> The trial by jury, or the country, *per patriam*, is also that trial by the peers of every Englishman, which as the grand bulwark of his liberties, is secured to him by the great charter....[1]

And, the Supreme Court of the United States said in 1898 that, "When Magna Carta declared no freeman should be deprived of life, etc., but by the judgment of his peers or by the law of the land, it referred to a trial by twelve jurors."[2]

The lawyers attending the American Bar Association meeting in London in July, 1971, pilgrimaged to Runnymede on Sunday, July 18, to relive a piece of history. The Chief Justice of the United States Supreme Court, Warren E. Burger, represented the American Bar Association and the Lord High Chancellor of Britain, Lord Hailsham, represented the English Bar. The Americans presented a piece of marble bearing the inscription, "18 July 1971, On this day, The American Bar Association again came here and pledged adherence to the Principle of the Great Charter." It will be recalled that the American Bar Association had made a similar pledge in 1957. Lord Hailsham commented upon the historical setting in which the charter was signed and noted its importance. He even displayed one of the four existing copies of the Magna Carta to those gathered for the occasion. Listening to these speeches and the conversation of the lawyers, both English and American, one gathered that the great charter was still widely revered among the legal profession for, among other things, guaranteeing jury trial.

49

However, in line with most modern authorities, Dawson does not support the popular opinion that Article 39 of the Magna Carta guarantees jury trial. He said,

> As originally used it [Article 39] was clearly not intended either as a generalized guaranty of jury trial or as a buttress for more ancient modes of community judging [reference to compurgation]. But it was expressed as a restraint of royal action, and despite the narrow meanings that were originally intended, clause 39 of Magna Carta deserves an honorable place in the history of constitutionalism. It was not till much later that "peers" were connected with jury trial.[3]

Dawson did concede that Article 39 "...projected 'judgment by peers across the sky of history for all the world to see."[4]

This concession is not enough. It is no doubt true that "peers" did not necessarily mean "jurors", but the impression left by Dawson's comments is that the Magna Carta had little or nothing to do with trial by jury and that it was only later that it was mistakenly assumed that trial by jury was guaranteed by the great charter. While it is true that the main purpose of the charter was to make the king subject to law, several provisions of the charter nonetheless referred to the right to trial by jury. Some of the following articles are indicative of this.

> 18. Assizes of novel disseisin, and of mort d' ancestor, and of darrien presentment, shall not be taken but in their proper counties, and after this manner: We, or, if we should be out of the realm, our chief justiciar, shall send two justiciaries through every county four times a year, who, with four knights, chosen out of every shire by the people, shall hold the said assizes, in the county on the day and at the place appointed for holding the assizes in each county, so many of the knights and freeholders as have been at the assizes aforesaid, shall stay to decide them as is necessary according as there is more or less business.

> 36. From henceforth nothing shall be given or taken for a writ of inquisition upon life or limbs, but it

shall be granted gratis, and shall not be denied.

39. No freeman shall be taken or imprisoned or disseised, or outlawed, or banished, or any ways destroyed, nor will we pass upon him, nor will we send upon him unless by the lawful judgment of his peers, or by the law of the land.

48. All evil customs concerning forests, warrens, foresters and warreners, sheriffs and their officers, rivers and their keepers, shall forthwith be inquired into each county, by twelve knights of the same shire, chosen by creditable persons of the same county; and with in forty days after said inquest, be utterly abolished, so as never to be restored: so as we are first acquainted therewith or our justiciary, if we should not be in England.[5]

A reading of the Magna Carta indicates that Article 36 is the one guaranteeing jury trial. If the word "inquisition" can be taken to mean "jury", then the phrase in Article 36 stating that, "...it shall be granted gratis, and shall not be denied" is particularly significant. The charter even presupposes the existence of the criminal jury.

The charter itself was almost immediately revoked by King John under the authority of the Pope, who held that it was void by reason of coercion. (The Pope's authority in English affairs resulted from the fact that King John had put his kindgom under the Pope's protection, although John received it back shortly before the barons forced him to sign the Magna Carta.) The relevant documents are on display at the British Museum. The charter, however, was reaffirmed by Henry III and is the first statute in the collection of British laws in force from 1225 until the present time.

Criminal juries existed prior to 1200,[6] but they were available only for a price, as this was before the Magna Carta.[7] Sometimes the money proved to have been wasted since there were convictions even by juries who were "had for a fee".[8] An example of a case with a happier result is the trial of one Randulph de Tottesworth who was charged with assault and battery. He gave King John a mark of silver for an inquisition of knights. The jury was granted, and Tottesworth was acquitted.[9]

From the reign of Richard I (1189-99) until the time of Edward in 1272, in the majority of cases the jury that had returned the indictment was also responsible for returning a verdict of guilt or innocence.[10] Even under these circumstances, there were occasional acquittals, as in the case of Robert Fitz, who was accused of illegally amercing (fining) tenants. The accusing jury was the trial jury and rendered a verdict of not guilty.[11] Generally, however, trial by these early juries meant almost certain conviction.[12]

Trials of criminal charges were still not ordinarily tried by jury in the early thirteenth century, and the Magna Carta did little to improve matters. What was to eventually have great effect on the use of jury trial in criminal cases was the decision by Pope Innocent III, at the Fourth Lateran Council, in November, 1215, forbidding the clergy to assist in the ordeals of water and fire.[13] This ruling was not implemented in England until a writ of Henry III early in 1219. That writ reads:

> The King to his beloved and faithful ... Justices Itinerant ... greetings: Because it was in doubt and not definitely settled before the beginning of your eyre, with what trial those are to be judged who are accused of robbery, murder, arson, and similar crimes, since the trial by fire and water has been prohibited by the Roman Church, it has been provided by our council that, at present, in this eyre of yours, it shall be done thus with those accused of excesses of this kind; To wit, that those who are accused of the aforesaid greater crimes, and of whom suspicion is held that they are guilty of that whereof they are accused, by whom also, in case they were permitted to abjure the real, still there would be suspicion that afterwards they would do evil, they shall be kept in our prison and safeguard, yet so that they do not incur danger of life or limb on our account. But those who are accused of medium crime, and to whom would be assigned the ordeal by fire or water, if it had not been prohibited, and

of whom, if they should adjure the realm there would
be no suspicion of their doing evil afterwards, they
may abjure our realm. But those who are accused of
lesser crimes, and of whom there would be no suspicion of evil, let them find safe and sure pledges of fi-
delity and of keeping our peace, and then they may be
released in our land.... We have left to your discretion
the observance of this aforesaid order ... according to
your own discretion and conscience. (dated Jan. 26,
1219).[14]

This writ does not spell out the mode of trial, no doubt leaving
it, in some measure, to the discretion of the judges. The king's
writ, however, and the Constitution of Clarendon made the jury
an obvious alternative by process of elimination.[15] In 1226, an
old woman was charged with a serious crime. Trial by battle was
therefore impossible due to her physical condition, in addition to
the fact that trial by battle itself was no longer in favor. She was
thus tried by jury.[16]

It was uncertain at the time of the king's writ whether or
not the defendant could be tried by a jury without his consent.
A number of persons had been tried by juries, convicted and
hung during the years 1220-22 who had never consented to a
jury trial. Actually, the demandant had never been required to
consent to a jury in the Grand Assize.[17] In addition, Wells gives
examples for the years 1220, 1222, and 1235 of defendants
being tried by juries without their consent.

One judge solved the dilemma by dispensing with trial altogether and hanging those accused, even though they had not
confessed and had not been caught in the act. He was fined for
this practice.[18] In 1284, a statute applicable to Wales solved the
problem in a limited way by declaring as guilty any person accused of personal trepass when damage was less than 40 shillings and the defendant refused to submit to trial by jury.[19] This
simple solution did not prevail, and by 1268 it was firmly established that the defendant must consent to trial by jury.[20] So it
was that the judges, in their comments to the jury, came to say,
"...and by this plea he hath put himself upon God and the country which country ye are."[21]

Obviously, the peace and order of society required that the guilt or innocence of those accused of crime be determined by some mode of trial. Criminals could not be allowed to escape punishment by the expedient of refusing to consent to jury trial. A statute was enacted in 1275 that helped solve the problem. It reads:

> Notorious felons, openly of ill fame, who will not put themselves on inquests for felonies with which they are charged before the justices at the king's suit, shall be put in strong and hard imprisonment as refusing the common law of the land. But this is not to be understood of persons who are taken on light suspicion.[22]

This statute became know as *prison forte et dure*. Wells suggests that the origin of this solution dates back to King Henry III's statute of 1219, quoted earlier in the chapter, which required the accused to be held in prison.[23] It is not surprising that most defendants did come to consent to trial by jury. Andrew Horne, the author of the *Mirror of Justices*, complained that persons were being compelled to be tried by their country, although they were willing to defend themselves against the charges by battle.[24]

Even this incentive to elect the jury was not deemed sufficient, and by 1291-92 additional provisions had been added to *prison forte et dure*. Thayer quotes Britton as to the fate of prisoners who refused to put themselves on their country at that time:

> ... barefooted, ungirt and bearheaded, in the worst place in the prison, upon the bare ground continually night and day, that they eat only bread made of barley or bran, and that they drink not, the day they eat, nor eat, the day they drink, nor drink anything but water and that they may be put in irons.[25]

The misfortunes of the recalcitrant prisoner escalated, and by 1302 the defendant was put in

> ...a house on the ground in his shirt, laden with as much iron as he could bear, and that he should have nothing to drink on the day when he had anything to

eat, and that he should drink water which came neither from fountain nor river.[26]

In keeping with these changes, the treatment was to be known
from this time forward as *peine forte et dure*, or, "pain, hard and
long." The specifics of this punishment varied, although invariably strong measures were believed to be necessary. Two
defendants in 1406 were to "...have iron as much and more
than they could bear...," and their water was to be "...standing
water from place nearest jail..."[27] A case in 1464 was similar except the prisoner was pressed with stones as well as with iron.
One woman managed to live 40 days under this treatment in
the middle of the fourteenth century.[28]

Such punishment as this before conviction makes one
curious as to what happened to those who were convicted.
About 1290, capital punishments included beheading, drawing,
hanging, burning alive, burying alive, falling from a dangerous
place, and so on. Corporal punishments could have included the
loss of an extremity; for example, a hand could be taken as punishment for stealing or the tongue for perjury, as well as beating
and imprisonment. Punishments also included forfeiture of pos-
sessions (moveable and otherwise), exile and ex-
communication.[29] Not all punishments were so drastic. It was
possible that the sentence could include labor on roads, pillory,
stocks, imprisonment or a simple pecuniary fine.[30] The possi-
bilities open to a judge of those days gave great room for the exercise of judicial discretion and imagination.

As has been noted in this chapter, the older accusatory jury
in many cases during the thirteenth century also assumed the
function of a trial jury. Thus, by the end of Henry III's reign in
1272, it was common for criminal cases to be submitted to the
presenting jury, the jury of another hundred, and to four town-
ships. These combined juries tried the case as a single body, and
a unanimous verdict was necessary. The number of these en-
larged juries ordinarily ranged from 24 to 84 members.

In the last years of the reign of Henry III and the early
years of the reign of Edward I, a method was used to appoint a
criminal court once the accusing court had returned an in-

dictment. The practice involved taking one member of the accusing jury to serve on the trial panel, along with members from other juries to make 12 jurors (the customary number in an accusing jury). Examples of this process in 1293 vary, however, with 2, 3, and 9 members having been selected from the accusing jury. In occasional cases, members from the accusing jury were not always chosen although in unusual situations as many as 14 jurors were chosen.[31] These jurors were usually knights,[32] and no oath was necessary, as the members had previously taken an oath as members of the accusing juries.

As late as 1340, it was thought to bode ill for the king if members of the accusing jury were not on the trial panel.[33] By a statute in the twenty-fifth year of the reign of Edward III, indictors were not permitted to remain on the trial jury if there was an objection by the defendant.[34] Even after this, it was the agents of the crown who picked the panel from which the jury was selected.[35]

At common law, where death was a possible penalty, the defendant was permitted to challenge 35 jurors, although the crown had no limit in the number of challenges. By a statute passed about the year 1305, the king's right to challenge was removed. However, this advantage to the defendant was invalidated, due to the fact that the crown was permitted to ask jurors to stand by until the panel was exhausted. There was no limit to the number that could be asked to stand by, and only if the panel was exhausted did the crown have to show cause.[36]

Wells summed up the development of criminal juries in four steps: (1) The accusing jury decided the mode of proof by which the defendant would clear himself; i.e., what kind of ordeal he must pass; (2) The accusing jury helped comprise the trial jury; (3) The accusing jury in addition to other jurors became the trial jury; and (4) A jury with new members, generally 12, was the trial jury.[37]

A verdict was accepted by the majority of the jurors as late as 1346,[38] but it was decided in 1367 that the verdict must be unanimous. The situation involved a case whereby a juror had refused to agree with the other 11 members of the court; he was sent to jail and the verdict of the other 11 had been accepted.[39] Other restrictions were also placed on the jury; for example, during the reign of Edward I (1272-1307), the jury was not permitted to eat and drink until their verdict had been received.[40] The privy verdict was in use by 1401, and could be returned by the jury after court had been adjourned for the day. After having delivered the verdict to the judge, the jurors could eat but had to verify the verdict in court the next day.[41]

A decision was made to cut off inquiry into the source of jury knowledge by 1300. Earlier, in 1224, a Jew named Bonamy Botun and his wife were accused of the murder of a Christian servant. Two juries were impanelled, one consisting of 12 Jews and the other of 18 Christians. The Jewish jury found him innocent and the Christian jury, on interrogation by the judge, also thought he was innocent, suspecting his family only. Dawson says, rightly, that if this type of interrogation had been permitted to develop it would have led to a canonist-civil law type of procedure.[42]

Forsyth claimed in 1852 that the criminal trial jury in the reign of Edward III (1327-1377) was "...nearly if not quite the same as at the present day."[43] This was not necessarily true, particularly with regard to criminal trial juries. For example, the defendant could not call witnesses although the crown could,[44] and the defendant was not permitted counsel.[45] In addition, a jury could be fined and imprisoned for a verdict in favor of the defendant,[46] although the reverse did not hold true.[47] It therefore seems impossible to agree with Forsyth's assessment after considering these major exceptions to his thesis.

Most of the preceding material in this chapter has concerned the criminal jury only. The procedure in civil trials came nearer to putting both plaintiff and defendant on an equal footing. Parties were permitted to be represented by counsel who were given a great deal of leeway. Counsel could make statements of fact to the jury, not necessarily based upon the evidence, and could exhibit unsealed writings to the jurors, while sealed writings could be taken into the jury room when the jury withdrew for deliberations.[48] By 1292, the judges were charging the jury much as in modern times.[49] In 1221, it was proper for

the parties to talk to the jury after they had retired.[50] By a statute of Edward I in 1285, juries were permitted to return a special verdict if they desired, whereupon the judge would determine the legal effect of the facts found.[51]

Juries are often popular in the abstract, but individuals are
seldom enthusiastic about serving on a jury themselves. This
was true in the thirteenth century as it is in the twentieth. In
1258, there were so many exemptions from jury service that
some counties had trouble finding enough knights to make up
the number needed for the Grand Assize.[52] Still, Edward I relieved freeholders whose land was not worth 20 shillings a year
from jury duty.[53] Also, it was held in the fourteenth century
that persons under the age of 21 could be witnesses but not jurors.[54]

A feature distinguishing the civil jury system from the
criminal was that a civil jury was subject to attaint, or punishment for a false verdict, while a criminal jury was not. It was
said that the procedure in criminal cases was so favorable to the
crown that it did not need attaint.[55] We have noted in Chapter
IV that jurors were punished for this conduct as early as the
time of Glanville (1181). The first judicial notice of such punishment was in 1202, and legislation concerning attaint has been
extant since 1268.[56] The scope of attaint expanded to include actions relating to real estate in 1275,[57] but about 1290 Andrew
Horne complained that it was still not as widely and easily available as it ought to be.[58] It was expanded again in 1327 to include
trespass, and by 1360 the jurors were subject to attaint in all
civil actions, both real and personal.[59]

If the 24 jurors of the attaint jury couldn't agree concerning
the accusation of a false verdict against the original trial jury,
they were afforced; i.e., members were added until there were
24 who could agree. If the attaint verdict went against the first
12, they were punished much as in the time of Glanville, but
with a few differences. All their land and personal property was
either destroyed or relinquished to the king, with their wives
and children left homeless, and they were thus declared "in-
famous" by the community, and held not "oathworthy" for future trials.[60]

The process by which the "modern" jury evolved, where jurors ceased to be witnesses and became judges of fact, began in the early thirteenth century and was largely, although not absolutely, completed by the end of the fourteenth century. The beginning of the change could be seen in a case of 1219 where a party "put himself on the jury and document witnesses."[61] These witnesses served as a constituent part of the trial jury, bridging the gap until the time when they would testify to the jury and not be a part of it. The witness nature of the jurors was emphasized when a writ to a sheriff ordered him to summon those persons present at a partition of property.[62] Generally in the thirteenth century, witnesses to deeds were summoned and deliberated with the jurors.[63] Also, jurors who had expert knowledge were summoned as jurors, once again highlighting the jurors' character as witnesses. In 1280, Florentines in London were summoned as jurors when the fact in issue had been done in Florence. In 1351, experts were summoned from particular trades when their special knowledge was useful in understanding a factual dispute. When a certificate was to be contradicted in 1363, merchants who best knew about it were summoned to serve on the jury.[64]

Process was issued for witnesses along with the jurors in 1218,[65] but the witnesses were so unessential that the taking of the inquest was not delayed or postponed for them.[66] And, in 1223, deed witnesses were still sitting with the jurors.[67] However, the distinction between the character of witnesses and that of jurors was beginning to be recognized even at this time. In 1338, witnesses could not be challenged. In 1349, the jury was charged to tell the truth to the best of its knowledge, while the witnesses were charged to tell the truth and to loyally inform the inquest.[68] The rule, effective by 1361, that deeds and documents had to be delivered in open court also aided in the evolution of the modern jury.[69] The first example of witness testimony being presented to the trial jury dates from 1371-75,[70] and by the end of the fourteenth century the character of the jurors as judges of the facts predominated over their role as witnesses.[71] This process had begun by separating the document witnesses from the jury, and this subsequently led the way to separating other witnesses. The process was complete for most purposes by 1460.[72]

During the thirteenth century there were a number of curious juries and trials. First of all, there continued to be trials in the original sense of the Frankish inquisitio. In 1248, the king directed a writ to the Mayor and citizens of London ordering them

> ...to elect twelve of the more discreet and lawful men of our city of London and join with them twelve good goldsmiths of the same city, making twenty-four discreet men in all, who shall go before the Barons of our Exchequer at Westminster and examine, upon oath, together with the barons, both the old and the new money of our land, and make provision how it may be bettered; and that it be made of good silver, and that it be lawful and for the good of the realm.[73]

This was the first form and instance of what was to become known as the trial of the Pyx, which we will return to in a later chapter.

Trial juries were almost uniformly coming to consist of 12 members, but juries that were in the nature of a public inquest did not necessarily conform to that number. The earliest statute enacted with regard to a coroner's inquest became effective in 1276. It directed that coroners, when required by a bailiff, the king or "honest men" of the county, summon five or six citizens and require them on oath to inquire into matters of violent death, treasure trove (concerning the property of the Crown), and housebreaking.[74]

In 1302, a knight objected to a jury picked to try him because the members were not knights; i.e., his peers. His objection was upheld, and when the knights were called, he was also permitted to object to the individual members.[75]

The jury *De Medietatem Linguae* was an extraordinary institution. It provided, by a charter granted by Edward I in 1303, that foreign merchants living within the kingdom should, in all cases in which they were involved except capital cases, be entitled to a jury trial which consisted of six foreign merchants resident in the city or town and six other good and lawful men of the place where the trial was to be held. If six foreign merchants could not be found, domestic merchants would serve in their place. There is a record of a foreign merchant in 1320 praying for a jury of 12 native and 12 foreign persons. The statute of 1303 was reaffirmed in 1353 with the additional provision that when both merchants were foreign the jury would be entirely foreign. This type of jury, with variations, was to be found in English law until the middle of the nineteenth century or later.[76] A similar principle was embodied in a statute of 1308 which directed a trial of ejectment in Shropshire to be tried by juries composed of half English and half Welsh.[77]

A case that occurred in 1356 would no doubt be a frightening prospect to modern citizens and lawyers alike. It consisted of a jury composed entirely of lawyers. A judge of the Common Pleas Bench had complained in the Court of the Exchequer that a woman had called him a "...traitor, felon and robber." The case was tried to a jury consisting of lawyers who practiced before the Court of Common Pleas.[78]

In 1219, we find a plaintiff proving his age by selecting 12 legal men, one of whom swore the plaintiff was of age. The other 11 persons selected swore that the oath of the first juror was true. This, of course, was a variation of compurgation. However, in 1397, there is an example of age being proved by a jury whose members were all 42 or older. The reason for requiring this age of the jurors was that they would all have been approximately 21 when the person whose age was in question was supposed to have been born.[79] This is reminiscent of the time when jurors functioned as witnesses as opposed to judges.

As to courts generally in the thirteenth century, the sheriff continued to hold court twice a year and preside at the county court once a month. A bailiff continued to preside over the court of the hundred every third week, and it functioned much like a county court.[80] Other courts of limited jurisdiction emerged more clearly in this century. There are clear records of the manor courts from 1237. They are very numerous toward the end of the thirteenth century and abundant in the fourteenth century.[81] Leet court was a local court similar to Baron's Court, with the distinction that the Leet court was interested in the community, as opposed to the business connected with a Baron's estate.[82] Leet juries and "homage" juries (form of jury in "Court Baron") sometimes served as local councils.[83] Justices of the peace were made custodians of the peace and were appointed by the king. They became stabilized by the fourteenth century, handling minor criminal matters. The local gentry got the appointments.[84] The private courts were somewhat hampered in adopting the jury system because of a statute of 1267 forbidding them to coerce freeholders to serve on juries against their will.[85] But local courts were eventually allowed to borrow the jury procedure for trial as well as for presentment.[86] Even justices of the peace were permitted to empanel juries to try the more serious cases.[87] Local courts were limited by a statute of 1278 to actions where the amount in controversy did not exceed 40 shillings, including the courts of hundreds and all other local courts.[88]

By 1300, the Court of Common Pleas had completed its separation from the Curia Regis and was stationary at Westminster.[89] In the thirteenth century, the Court of Common Pleas had seven or eight judges, while the King's Bench had three. The fact-finding part of the court's work consisted of dispatching commissions to local gentry who were required to preside, receive verdicts and render judgments. These commissions came to be known in the thirteenth century as commissions of "oyer" and "terminer" (to hear and determine). In 1273, there were 2,000 commissions of assize. A royal judge was not always a member of the commission, but it was common for one royal judge to preside with other members of the commission including local nobles, clergy and the like. The circuit court became similar to but more important than the county courts.[90]

During these two centuries, trial by jury had become the dominant mode of trial. This did not mean that the older modes of trial had died altogether. For example, an interesting type of compurgation took place in the thirteenth century. In an action for a debt, the person who had the burden of proof brought 10 witnesses to the trial with him. Five were lined up on one side and five on the other. A knife was thrown into the ground between the two lines. A man was selected from the five on the side toward which the handle of the knife inclined. One of the five selected was removed and the other four took on oath as compurgators.[91] In an action for trespass in 1304, a party offered combat and the opposite party accepted it but the court refused to permit it.

The thirteenth and fourteenth centuries saw many significant developments in the jury procedures. The next four centuries were to see the most significant development of all. The jury would be transformed into a just mode of trial.

Chapter V Footnotes

1. *Commentaries On the Laws of England,* William Blackstone, Esq. (4 Vols, 7th Ed., Oxford, 1775, 1st Ed. 1765), IV-349.

2. *Thompson* v. *Utah,* 170 U.S. 343 (1898).

3. *A History of Lay Judges,* John P. Dawson (Harvard Univ. Press, Cambridge, Mass., 1960), pp. 289-90.

4. *Id.* at p. 289.

5. *Federal Code Annotated* (Bobbs-Merrill Co., 1950), Constitution Vol., pp. 3-4.

6. *History of Trial by Jury,* William Forsyth (London, 1852), pp. 200-01.

7. *The Origin of Juries,* Heinrich Brunner (Berlin, 1872), p. 472.

8. "Early Opposition to Petty Juries in Criminal Cases," Charles L. Wells, 30 Law Q. Rev. 97 (1914) at p. 102.

9. Forsyth, *op. cit.* at note 6, at p. 201.

10. "The Origin of the Petty Jury," Charles L. Wells, 27 Law Q. Rev. 347 (1911), at p. 350.

11. Forsyth, *op. cit.* at note 6, at p. 200.

12. *The Proof of Guilt,* Glanville Williams (Stevens and Sons, London, 1963), pp. 4-5; and Wells, *op. cit.* at note 8, at p. 101.

13. Wells, *op. cit.* at note 8, at p. 98.

14. Wells, *op. cit.* at note 10, at p. 352.

15. *A History of Lay Judges,* John P. Dawson (Harvard Univ. Press, Cambridge, Mass. 1960), p. 293.

16. *A Preliminary Treatise on Evidence,* James Bradley Thayer (Sweet and Maxwell, London, 1898), pp. 70-71.

17. *Id.* at p. 70.

18. Thayer, *op. cit.* at note 16, at p. 72.

19. Thayer, *op. cit.* at note 16, at p. 78.

20. Wells, *op. cit.* at note 8, at p. 104.

21. *Trial By Jury,* Sir Patrick Devlin (Stevens and Sons, London, 3rd ed. 1966, 1st ed. 1956), p. 16.

22. Thayer, *op. cit.* at note 16, at p. 74.

23. Wells, *op. cit.* at note 10, at p. 352.

24. *The Mirror of Justices,* Andrew Horne, translated by William Hughes 1646, (London, 1768), p. 227.

25. Thayer, *p. cit.* at note 16, at pp. 74-75.

26. Thayer, *op. cit.* at note 16, at p. 75.

27. Thayer, *op. cit.* at note 16, at p. 75.

28. Thayer, *op. cit.* at note 16, at pp. 75-76.

29. Horne, *op. cit.* at note 24, at pp. 190-91, 193-94.

30. Horne, *op. cit.* at note 24, at p. 206.

31. Wells, *op. cit.* at note 10, at pp. 354-58.

32. Thayer, *op. cit.* at note 16, at p. 71.

33. Thayer, *op. cit.* at note 16, at p. 83.

34. Wells, *op. cit.* at note 16, at p. 361.

35. *A History of English Law,* Sir William Holdsworth (Sweet and Maxwell, London, 7th Ed. 1956, 1st Ed. 1903), I-325-26.

36. Forsyth, *op. cit.* at note 6, at pp. 231-33.

37. Wells, *op. cit.* at note 16, at p. 359.

38. Holdsworth, *op. cit.* at note 35, I-318.

39. Devlin, *op. cit.* at note 21, at p. 48.

40. Forsyth, *op. cit.* at note 6, at p. 243.

41. Holdsworth, *op. cit.* at note 35, I-319.

42. Dawson, *op. cit.* at note 15, at pp. 124, 126.

43. Forsyth, *op. cit.* at note 6, at p. 207.

44. Williams, *op. cit.* at note 12, at p. 5.

45. *The Jury,* W.R. Cornish (Penguin Press, London, 1968), p. 72.

46. Holdsworth, *op. cit.* at note 35, at I-326.

47. Thayer, *op. cit.* at note 16, at p. 112.

48. Thayer, *op. cit.* at note 16, at pp. 103, 107-08.

49. Thayer, *op. cit.* at note 16, at p. 112.

50. Thayer, *op. cit.* at note 16, at p. 110.

51. Forsyth, *op. cit.* at note 6, at p. 260.

52. *The History of English Law,* Sir Frederick Pollock and Frederic Maitland (Cambridge Univ. Press, 1898), II-631.

53. *Id.* at II-631-2.

54. Holdsworth, *op. cit.* at note 35, at I-336.

55. *Id.* at I-341.

56. Thayer, *op. cit.* at note 16, at p. 141.

57. Holdsworth, *op. cit.* at note 35, at I-339-40.

58. Horne, *op. cit.* at note 24, at p. 235-36.

59. Holdsworth, *op. cit.* at note 35, at I-339-40.

60. Forsyth, *op. cit.* at note 6, at pp. 181-83.

61. Thayer, *op. cit.* at note 16, at p. 95.

62. Thayer, *op. cit.* at note 16, at p. 102.

63. Holdsworth, *op. cit.* at note 35, at I-334.

64. Thayer, *op. cit.* at note 16, at p. 94.

65. Holdsworth, *op. cit.* at note 16, at I-334.

66. Thayer, *op. cit.* at note 16, at p. 101.

67. Thayer, *op. cit.* at note 16, at p. 103.

68. Thayer, *op. cit.* at note 16, at p. 100.

69. Holdsworth, *op. cit.* at note 35, at I-334.

70. Thayer, *op. cit.* at note 16, at p. 123.

71. Holdsworth, *op. cit.* at note 16, at I-319.

72. Brunner, *op. cit.* at note 7, at p. 436.

73. "Royal Mint Annual Report for 1963," Royal Mint (London 1963), p. 5.

74. Forsyth, *op. cit.* at note 6, at p. 226.

75. Holdsworth, *op. cit.* at note 16, at I-324.

76. Forsyth, *op. cit.* at note 6, at pp. 228-30.

77. Forsyth, *op. cit.* at note 6, at p. 230.

78. Thayer, *op. cit.* at note 16, at p. 93.

79. Thayer, *op. cit.* at note 16, at p. 19.

80. Dawson, *op. cit.* at note 3, at pp. 182, 133, 178.

81. Dawson, *op. cit.* at note 3, at pp. 192, 198.

82. Dawson, *op. cit.* at note 3, at pp. 200, 221.

83. Dawson, *op. cit.* at note 3, at p. 244.

84. Dawson, *op. cit.* at note 3, at p. 136.

85. Dawson, *op. cit.* at note 3, at pp. 185-86.

86. Dawson, *op. cit.* at note 3, at p. 296.

87. Dawson, *op. cit.* at note 3, at p. 139.

88. Dawson, *op. cit.* at note 3, at p. 180.

89. Forsyth, *op. cit.* at note 6, at p. 168.

90. Dawson, *op. cit.* at note 3, at pp. 129-32.

91. Thayer, *op. cit.* at note 16, at p. 26.

VI
Tudor Oppression: Georgian Justice
1400-1789

During this period, a criminal defendant could answer an indictment either by demurrer or by a plea of "not guilty."[1] Although specific evidence was not always consistent with the charge as contained in the indictment, the jury could convict on contradictory evidence as long as it was received at least one day before action was commenced.[2]

It was still difficult for the defendant to refuse to accept a trial by jury. *Peine forte et dure* was still an effective remedy for recalcitrancy. Two who were charged with robbery in 1406 were said to be "Mute of malice [to] delay their death." It was ordered that they undergo *peine forte et dure* "so to the death."[3] At Newgate Prison in London, 1662, George Harley was indicted for robbery and refused to plead. His thumbs were tied together with whipcord so the pain would compel him to submit to a jury.[4] Burnwater was accused of murder in 1728 and refused to plead. He was pressed for one and three-fourths hours under 400 pounds of iron. He changed his mind, pleaded not guilty, was tried by a jury, convicted and hung.[5] Tying the thumbs with whipcord continued at Newgate until at least 1734. This prison also added the refinement to *peine forte et dure* by placing either a stake or sharp stone under the prisoner's neck.[6]

The year 1772 was to see the end of *peine forte et dure*, as it was abolished by statute. After that time, the accused either stood as convicted by his refusal to plead,[7] or his refusal to plead was taken as a plea of not guilty.[8] For example, on a charge of treason, a refusal to plead was equivalent to conviction except when insanity was suspected. In such a case, it was left to a jury to decide whether the defendant remained silent to avoid punishment, or whether he did so rightfully by "the providence of God."[9]

When the defendant's plea was entered and a writ of *venire facias* (order for the jury panel to be summoned) had been issued, it was up to the sheriff to return the jurors. If he excused anyone under the age of 70, he was subject to a fine of 20 pounds to be recovered by the person bringing the charge.[10] If the sheriff was not impartial, the panel was returned by the coroner. If the coroner in turn was not impartial, the judges nominated two persons to direct the process.[11]

The requirements as to the composition of the jury varied from time to time. In 1543-44, a statute set forth that only six members of the panel need be from the hundred. This was reduced to two in 1584-85,[12] and, in 1705, it was sufficient that the jurors be from the county.[13] The general requirements for the selection of jurors was that they be peers or equals, and 21 to 70 years of age; not outlawed, attainted or convicted of treason, felony, perjury, conspiracy or adjudged to the pillory; not an alien (unless an alien was being tried); and in general the most highly respected members of the community were selected.[14] At common law there was no requirement that the freehold of a juror be of a certain value, and jurors in cities and towns were not required to have a freehold at all, although there would be a monetary requirement; e.g., 100 marks in London (a mark is equal to 12 shillings and four pence).[15] In the English Bill of Rights (1688), it was complained that jurors had been chosen in cases for high treason who were not freeholders.[16] If the case involved a capital offense, a juror was required to have a freehold in the county worth 40 shillings a year.[17] A statute of 1751 eliminated the requirement that there be a knight on the panel.[18]

In some cases, qualified jurors might be exempt from serving on juries. Jurors were exempt if they had served on a jury within the previous year in the same jurisdiction, or within the previous four years in the county of York.[19] A member of any holy order, a sailor or an apothecary living in London or within seven miles of the city were exempt from jury service. By a statute of 1696, no Quaker could serve on a jury because his religion prevented him from taking the oath.[20]

A party could challenge both the array (entire panel returned by the sheriff) or the polls (individual jurors).[21] At common law, in cases of high treason or felony, the defendant had 35 challenges. This was reduced in 1531 to only 20. If a party challenged a greater number than allowed, he was "put on his penance"; i.e., the *peine forte et dure*.[22] The king had no peremptory challenges,[23] although both sides could challenge for cause. The following reasons were judged to be sufficient causes: (1) the juror had been on the grand jury which had indicted the defendant (criminal case); (2) the juror was a serf or servant; (3) the juror had been convicted of certain crimes; (4) he was related to one of the parties or to the sheriff[24] (a degree of relationship could be objectionable to the ninth degree);[25] (5) the juror had an action pending against a party; (6) the juror would benefit by judgment to be rendered; and (7) the juror had served as an arbitrator in the matter, or had declared his opinion on the question to be submitted.[26]

In the case of challenge to the array, two individuals (perhaps two attorneys or two coroners) were appointed by the judge to hear the case. In a challenge to polls, the judge again selected two persons to hear the case, and the polls were tried two at a time until all challenges were settled.[27] As has been discussed, although the king had no peremptory challenges, he could ask an unlimited number of jurors to stand aside, and the king did not have to show cause unless the panel was exhausted. After a juror was sworn, he could not be challenged except for cause occurring after he was sworn.[28] In the sixteenth century, the various parties were often able to interview individual jurors to determine their fitness to hear the case. A list of prospective jurors could be obtained from the sheriff,[29] and ordinarily jurors were selected from the panel by lot.[30]

After the jurors or a portion of them were selected, a view of the scene by the jurors could be had in most actions involving real property. When it was decided to have a view, at least six jurors were selected either by the consent of the parties involved or chosen by the judge. Upon completion of the view and by the day set for trial, enough other jurors were added to make 12.[31]

In the fifteenth and sixteenth centuries, the parties had a

right not only to question the jurors for the purpose of obtaining information on which to base challenges, but they also had a right to inform the jurors of their position before the day of trial.[32] This right was incorporated in a statute of 1427 which provided that, upon request, the parties would be given a list of the jurors six days before the trial so as to "...inform them of their right and title before the day of the session".[33] In a letter to Sir Richard Plumpton in 1498-99, the writer recited that he had previously sent a copy of the panel of jurors to Sir Plumpton and continued,

> Therefore, Sir, between you and my lady ye must cause special labor to be made, so it be downe prevely, to such of the Jurrours, as ye trust wilbe made frindly in the cause.[34]

In another letter, Sir Richard was urged,

> ...to make labor to them that they appeare not, or else to be favorable to you according to right, and enform them of the matter as well as ye can for their consciences.[35]

But, in 1682, it was punishable to use this technique in order to influence the jury's verdict.[36]

If enough jurors were not left after challenges to make up 12, it was permissible to appoint tales; i.e., persons on the spot at the courthouse who were pressed into service. They are first mentioned in the year 1544.[37] In the past, the parties could even challenge a judge, but this ceased to be permitted under Justice Coke (1552-1634).[38] Perhaps the right to challenge the judge was not as necessary after 1700 when judges no longer served at the pleasure of the crown, but for life or good behavior.[39]

The prohibition against jurors eating and drinking continued in force. A statute of Henry VIII, issued in 1535 without the sanction of Parliament, directed the officer in charge of the jurors to keep them from eating, drinking and talking with others.[40] It was especially undesirable if the jurors had their nourishment at the expense of one of the parties, and the jurors could be challenged for this.[41] In one case in 1588, jurors were searched for food by the officer in charge. Two were found to have some figs, having eaten some, while three jurors were found with apples but had not eaten any. Those with the figs were fined five pounds each, and those with the apples were fined 40 shillings each. The verdict which they had returned was found to be good, however.[42] The reign of Elizabeth I seems to have been less severe than that of her father's reign (Henry VIII). During his reign jurors who ate apples were not only fined five pounds each but were committed to the fleet.[43]

The jury could eat and drink after delivering a privy verdict to the judge after he had risen for the day, but had to affirm their verdict in open court the next day.[44] In one case, an enterprising solicitor (lawyer) paid the bill for wine which a jury, while deliberating in a tavern, had ordered before returning a privy verdict. After the privy verdict in his client's favor was given to the judge, the solicitor again treated the jury at the tavern. The bill for both the wine and the rest of the celebration was not paid until after the verdict was given to the judge. (The verdict was good.)[45] With the permission of the justices, the jurors were permitted to eat, even at the cost of the parties, if they agreed. After the conclusion of a trial at Old Bailey in London, England, in October and November, 1971, the victorious defendants (the "Notting Hill Gate eight") and jurors had refreshments at a nearby public house. A month later, one of the defendants treated the jury and others to a party at a restaurant which he owned.

Criminal defendants were not generally permitted the assistance of counsel during this time, even though the crown might have as many as four lawyers.[46] Counsel were permitted for the purpose of arguing law to the court by 1681. In fact, it was suggested at that time that the court ought to appoint counsel for that purpose if necessary and the defendant desired it.[47] The author to A Guide to English Juries gives us the reason for not permitting defendants charged with crime to be represented by counsel. Quoting from a trial, he says:

> The only Reason ... why a prisoner is allowed no
> councel in matter of Fact or in any thing but matter in
> law, when life or member is concerned, is only this,
> the Evidence whereby he shall be condemned, ought to

be so plain and evident, that all the councel in the
world may be presumed able to say nothing against it
or in his defense.[48]

In 1752, it was still generally the law that the defendant could
not have counsel, although treason and misprision had been excepted from this practice by statute since 1696. The reason for
this practice was that it was felt that the judge ought to be the
prisoner's counsel.[49] By the eighteenth century, defense counsel
were permitted to cross-examine witnesses.[50]

Among other obstacles facing the criminal defendant, he
was not permitted to testify in his own behalf.[51] His wife was
also not permitted to testify except as to certain offenses such as
offenses against his children or his wife.[52] Ordinarily, however,
the wife could not be a witness against her husband.[53] It wasn't
until the seventeenth century that the defendant was permitted
to call any witnesses,[54] although a statute in 1606 gave the accused the right to have witnesses under oath in certain felony
cases.[55] Apart from statute, several witnesses in one case testified for a defendant in 1632, but they were not sworn.[56] It became the usual practice for the defendant to call witnesses after
1640, although they were still not permitted to be sworn.[57] In
fact, in one case in 1679, Chief Justice Coke refused to let witnesses for the defendant be sworn,[58] and actually even crown
witnesses were not always sworn by the mid century.[59] By the
late 1600's, however, the judges had come to the view that unsworn testimony was no evidence at all,[60] and by the eighteenth
century the defendant's witnesses were finally allowed to be
sworn.[61] Another problem in court procedure was that ordinarily court papers were in Latin, although during Cromwell's time
English was used.[62] When necessary, the papers were read to
the jurors in English.[63]

In addition to other problems, a witness had to contend
with the threat of physical violence from the party opposed to
his testimony.[64] He could also be compelled to attend court from
as early as the mid sixteenth century.[65] If the witness volun-
teered his testimony without process, he was also subject to a
charge of maintenance, a crime dating back as early as 1433.[66]
The Star Chamber decided in 1562-63 that a witness could be

punished for perjury, but excepted those cases where there had been a conviction for a felony or murder. This court didn't want to deter witnesses for the king from coming forth.[67]

The courts established elaborate rules of evidence to control what the jury would hear. The most familiar of these rules is that excluding hearsay evidence, which was invented about 1700.[68] Even before the judge summed up, it invalidated the verdict if the jury separated and it could be punished for violation of this rule.[69] Judges had charged the jury long before 1400, and were allowed to give their opinions on the case.[70] The judge did not leave all the facts for the jurors, however; one jury decided, in 1597, for example, that certain articles of clothing could not be necessities for an infant as a matter of law.[71] If the jury was unable to reach a verdict before the court had to continue on its circuit to the next town, the court would have the jurors put in a cart, and they would be carried around the circuit with the judge until they reached a decision.[72] Instead of returning a general verdict, the jury could return a special verdict; i.e., specially finding the fact in dispute and leaving it for the judge to apply the law.[73] The King's Bench began ordering special venires (panels of jurors) of high or special standing in the late seventeenth century.[74] The procedure for selecting a special jury consisted of the sheriff and parties attending an officer of the court who would name 48 freeholders. Each side struck 12 alternately, one at a time, the plaintiff beginning. If a party didn't appear, 12 were stricken for him. There were no special juries in capital cases because the defendant would have been deprived of his peremptory challenges.[75] One of the early special juries was convened in 1645-46 in the King's Bench, consisting of merchants who were to try an issue between two other merchants concerning their business affairs.[76] An inquiry held in 1730 disclosed that special juries had been ordered in cases presenting difficult issues without the consent of the parties, but only prior to 1700.[77] A statute of 1730, amended in 1751, provided that any person who applied for a special jury could have it upon payment of the expense for striking it, and all additional expense occasioned thereby. No allowance was to be made in the costs for this expense unless the judge ruled the case a proper one to be tried to a special jury. The statute provided that the special jurors were to be paid a reasonable sum not to exceed one pound and one shilling (a guinea, hence the name "guinea men"), unless a view was necessary.[78]

Quite apart from attaint, jurors were subject to punishment by the contempt power of the court. For example, jurors could be punished for receiving a paper from a party after retiring for deliberation. In 1410, a verdict was set aside for this specific reason.[79] In 1585 a verdict was set aside when it was discovered that the jury had examined a witness in private after retiring, although in another case the verdict was held good after both parties had delivered a paper to the jury by mutual consent.[80] Verdicts were set aside in 1675, 1677 and 1722 because the jurors had cast lots to arrive at verdicts. In the 1677 case, the offense was proved by affidavit of a juror.[81]

The law courts copied the Star Chamber in fining and imprisoning jurors who refused to convict.[82] A rare exception to the contrary was a case in 1500 in which a judge was fined for imprisoning a jury that had refused to convict.[83] A statute of 1534, applicable to Wales and the marches only, authorized the fining and imprisoning of jurors.[84] A similar statute applicable to England was issued without authority of Parliament by King Henry VIII in 1535. It provided that if the jurors acquitted felons contrary to the weight of the evidence or otherwise "misbehaved", they could be fined and imprisoned at the discretion of the court. This act was soon declared illegal,[85] although the practice continued. Cases are recorded in 1535 and 1554 of juries being fined on failure to convict, [86] and from 1571 to 1597 jurors were frequently fined for finding contrary to the direction of the court.[87] During the years 1664-65, jurors insisted on acquitting Quakers of various charges and were fined for their actions. The judges of the Common Bench generally agreed that this practice of fining was unlawful, although it nonetheless continued, and more jurors continued to be punished in 1666 and 1667.[88]

A resolution of the Commons, dated December 13, 1667, declared, "That the precedents and practice of fining or imprisoning jurors, for verdicts is illegal."[89] Not surprisingly, there is

no record, according to Williams, of punishing jurors for conviction.[90] At long last, the practice came to a permanent halt
with Bushell's case in 1670.[91] After that, jurors could be punished for ministerial acts only.[92] The jury did have some protection under the law, however. An irate party, having lost his
case, assaulted a juror and was sentenced to life imprisonment.[93]

The Star Chamber, a criminal court which had extraordinary powers, was composed of members of the king's privy
council. It did not use a jury.[94] The Star Chamber and its powers
are described in a work written in 1764.

> ...Henry the 7th, one of the worst Princes this nation
> ever knew, procured an act of Parliament which, after
> reciting many defects and abuses in trials by Jury, and
> pretending a remedy for the same, gives a summary
> jurisdiction to certain great officers of state, taking to
> their aid a bishop, to summon, try and punish of their
> own mere discretion and authority, any persons who
> shall be accused of the offenses therein very generally
> named and described. In short, the court of the Star
> Chamber is, by this act, so enlarged in its jurisdiction,
> that it may be said to be erected, and both grand and
> petit Juries in crown matters are in great measure laid
> aside...[95]

The Star Chamber used torture to extract confessions,[96]
and it was apt to treat as corrupt any verdict of acquittal which
it considered as against the weight of the evidence. There are
many examples of this court punishing jurors with fines and imprisonment for this offense during the reigns of Henry VIII,
Mary and Elizabeth I.[97] There are even rare fines imposed for
verdicts of acquittal,[98] and in all cases the penalties could be
heavy. The foreman and another juror from the jury acquitting
Throctmorton in 1554 were fined 2,000 pounds each and committed to prison. Six of the jurors were fined 1,000 marks each
and sent to prison, while four members of this jury admitted
they had been in the wrong and were released.[99] Edmund Burke
insisted that although the Star Chamber was abolished in 1635,
its maxims continued to persist.[100]

Although testimony by witnesses appearing before the jury was to be the chief source of evidence, the jurors themselves, to a lesser degree, were also permitted to testify. In 1472, a statute of Edward IV provided that process for witnesses was not to issue unless it was requested.[101] Considering that witnesses were subject to fine for volunteering, this probably meant that if no process was issued, there would be no evidence other than the private knowledge of the jurors. The last record of deed witnesses being summoned with the jury is in 1489.[102] Justice Vavaseur, in 1499, decided that the jury could bring in a verdict even if no evidence was offered.[103] It was held in 1598 that a juror could communicate his private knowledge to the other jurors.[104] Even though it was discovered, in 1599, that a juror had taken a paper into deliberation with him and had shown it to the other jurors, the verdict was held to be good.[105] The court said, during the trial of Nathaniel Reading in 1679, that jurors were not strangers to the facts, but if they had evidence to offer, they ought to be sworn as jurors.[106] This was similar to a case of 1650, the only difference being that, in the earlier case, the juror was not required to take an oath as a witness in addition to this oath as a juror.[107]

However, Brunner makes reference to a statute of 1650 which further differentiates between the roles of witness and jurors.[108] It was held improper for a jury to approve a deed that had not been pleaded or given in evidence.[109] These authorities notwithstanding, Blackstone nonetheless declared in 1765 that there were two kinds of evidence — that given in proof and the private knowledge of the jurors.[110]

The practice of granting new trials in civil cases was claimed by one justice to have been an ancient tradition, while another claimed that the practice originated in 1652.[111] Perhaps this passage from the *Plumpton Correspondence,* written before 1523, is evidence of an early new trial:

> ...in which drytinge is conteyned how the Justices of
> the Common Place awarded a new *venire facias* betwyxt
> my master your son and William Babthorpp...[112]

This second panel could have been ordered because of some defect in procedure before the completion of the first trial. Most authorities, however, agree that the first instance of calling a new trial in a civil case was ordered in 1655 in the case of *Wood* v *Gunston*. The action was libel, and the ground for the new trial was excessive damages of 1,500 pounds.[113] In any event, it became common in the last of the seventeenth century to set aside the initial civil verdict and to call a new trial on various grounds,[114] such as: lack of notice, variance, want of a proper jury, misbehavior of a party, new evidence, surprise testimony, absence of a witness or attorney, subsequent conviction of a witness for perjury, misdirection of the jury by the judge, verdict not supported by evidence, misbehavior of jurors, and excessive damages.[115]

As to criminal trials, in two cases in 1660, new trials were ordered in favor of the king after verdicts of acquittal.[116] New trials were ordered in favor of the defendants in cases in 1673 and 1681 after a charge of perjury had been brought and proved concerning the original trials.[117] Justice Hawkins said, in 1621, that a verdict against the crown could not be set aside, although one against the defendant could.[118] The defendant, however, could not get a new trial after conviction of a capital crime, the only known exception to this taking place in 1851.[119] In 1752, it was uncertain whether the crown, at the close of the evidence, could withdraw a juror and have the cause retried. The anonymous author of *The Complete Juryman* concluded that it could not be done in capital cases and was permissible in other cases only with the consent of both parties.[120]

The procedure of a civil trial as it might have taken place in 1752 is briefly described in *The Complete Juryman*.[121] The names of the jurors were first drawn and they were sworn to this oath, "You shall well and truly try this Issue between the parties, and a true Verdict give, according to the Evidence. So help you God." When 12 were selected, the plaintiff opened with his witnesses (assuming he had the burden of proof) and the defense was permitted to cross-examine them. Then the defendant produced his witnesses after which the plaintiff was permitted to reply. The judge summed up, the jury retired and returned with the verdict. The judge rendered judgment accordingly. Attorneys of today would obviously not find this procedure unfamiliar.

On a charge of high treason, the procedure was somewhat different.[122] The jurors were called, challenged and sworn. The bailiff called for anyone who could inform on the charge, and the king's counsel thus opened his case. All witnesses endorsed on the back of the indictment were sworn by the clerk. This was the oath:

> The Evidence which you and every of you shall give to the court and Jury not sworn, for our Sovreign Lord the King, against the Prisoner at the Bar, shall be the Truth, the whole Truth, and nothing but the Truth. So help you God.

The defendant was permitted to cross-examine the king's witnesses and, in his turn, to question his own witnesses. The king had the right to present rebuttal. Both the prisoner and counsel for the king presented arguments and the Chairman (presiding judge) summed up the case. Then the clerk had the crier swear the bailiff:

> You shall well and truly keep this Jury without meat, drink, Fire or Candle; (if it be in the night-time, the word candle is to be omitted) You shall not suffer any person to speak unto them nor you yourself, unless to ask them, whether they are agreed of their Verdict, until they shall be agreed of their verdict. So help you God.

The jurors were then taken to a private and convenient room. They were not permitted to give a privy verdict in a case of treason. When they returned, the judge addressed them, "You of the Jury look upon the prisoner; how say you, is A.D. guilty of the High Treason of which he stands indicted, or not guilty."

If the verdict was "guilty" and the defendant was a woman, she was asked what she could say to stay execution. If she claimed to be pregnant, a panel of matrons, "12 good and motherly women," was selected "...to handle and inspect her Body and secret Parts." They were sworn to "...enquire, search and try whether the prisoner be quick with child." The oath was again given to the bailiff with the difference that it provided for the prisoner retiring with the matrons.[123] This seems to be the only jury of women in the history of the English jury, at least before the twentieth century.

In the years previous to the middle of the nineteenth century, executions were a public affair. A passage from the *Plumpton Correspondence* gives some idea of what was involved in this ceremony. The following is a reference to persons recently convicted of treason:

> ...they should be drawn on hirdiles from the Tower, throwout London, to the Tyburne, and there to be hanged, and cut down quicke, and ther bowels to be taken out and burned; their heads to be strike of, and quartered, ther head and quarters to be disposed at the Kyngs pleasure.[124]

It is to be assumed that the King would have the heads and quarters displayed from gibbets, or stakes, along the public highways to discourage future evil conduct.

Attaint, or the punishment of jurors for rendering a false verdict, continued to be used during this period. Although knights were no longer required on ordinary juries, it remained the practice to have a knight among the 24 members of the attaint jury.[125] The early punishment heaped upon the convicted jurors (namely, forfeiture of goods, "chattels," lands and tenements to the king; wife and children thrust out of doors; houses razed and thrown down; meadows plowed and bodies thrust into prison) was somewhat ameliorated by a statute of 1490 which provided for a 20 pound fine to be divided between the king and the prosecuting party, plus a ransom and fine at the discretion of the judge. In addition, the attainted party could never be a witness in court, and the party damaged by the first verdict was restored to what he had lost. If the matter had involved less than 40 pounds, the fine was to be five pounds only. But, it seems that a party could elect to bring the attaint action under either the common law procedure or this statute.[12] A provision restricted to London and dating from 1495 limited the punishment for attaint to a 20 pound fine or more and imprisonment for six months or less, in addition to being forever forbidden to be a witness in court.

In 1542, it was held that the only evidence which could be presented to the attaint jury was that which had been submitted to the original jury.[127] If, however, the original jurors chose, they could give evidence of private knowledge which they had had at the time they gave the original verdict. If they chose to submit such evidence the party bringing the attaint could offer evidence in rebuttal[128]. This practice was more frequently used when the roles of juror and witness were more closely intertwined; after the middle of the sixteenth century, attaint was seldom used.[129]

As has been noted in an earlier chapter, the form of the early inquests left the members little room to decide questions of law. When inquests or juries began to be used more extensively in criminal cases to judge guilt or innocence, they had the power, if not the right, to decide questions of law as well as fact. This is still true today. This situation was not quite the same with respect to civil trials. In those cases, the judge had a much greater control over the result by means of such devices as the demurrer, summary judgment, directed verdict, judgment notwithstanding the verdict, new trials, remittiturs, admittiturs and much more.

It is probable in England that the juries were far too intimidated until the last third of the seventeenth century to presume to judge anything except that which the justices told them to judge, and we can be reasonably sure the justices kept them to the facts alone. At that time, however, there was great dissatisfaction with the quality of royal justice, and a look was given to the jury's power to decide law as well as facts. In *The Security of Englishmen's Lives*, Lord Somers, Lord High Chancellor of England under King William, said in 1681:

> As it hath been the law, so it hath always been the custom, and practice of these juries, upon all general issues, pleaded in cases civil as well as criminal, to judge both of the law and fact.[130]

His was not an isolated opinion. Sir John Hawles in 1771 stated his opinion that law should be the prerogative of the judge and facts should be left to the jury, although the jury resolves law and fact in a general verdict.[131] Part of the judge's job, according to Hawles, was to sum up fact and law, but without binding the jury.[132] Justice Holt said, in 1697,

> ...that in all cases and in all actions the jury may give a general or special verdict, as well in causes criminal as civil, and the court ought to receive it, if it is pertinent to the issue, for if the jury doubt they may refer themselves to the court, but are not bound so to do....[133]

Thus, in 1704, Justice Holt submitted not only the fact of publication of a libel and the identity of the persons in question to the jury, but the issue of criminality as well.[134]

In spite of these opinions in favor of the jury's right as well as its power to decide law, the following could be thought of as an accurate description of the state of English law in 1752:

> A question of law is not capable of being decided by any, but by those, who are learned in the Law: and therefore it is always to be determined by the Judges; but a Question of fact is for the most part to be tried by a Jury of twelve men....[135]

In addition,

> If the Jury will take upon themselves the knowledge of the law, they may give a general verdict, but it is dangerous for them so to do; for if they mistake the law they run into the danger of an attaint; therefore, where the case is doubtful, it is safest for them to find the special matter.[136]

Under this view, if the jurors decided law, they were exercising a power, not a right. They would therefore be subject to punishment for attaint, which would not be true if they were exercising a right.

Contrary to this, Pettingal, writing in 1769, said that juries should have "power of Judgment in themselves."[137] Although Pettingal may in some instances be considered a "romantic,"

Lord Camden in the eighteenth century agreed, and was a strong advocate of this position throughout his career as defense attorney, attorney general, and upon the bench. In a speech in the House of Lords in 1770, he took exception to an opinion of Lord Mansfield's doctrine that denied the jury the right to decide the law in cases of libel. In his last speech in the House of Lords in 1792, in the debate on Fox's libel bill, he said:

> ...the jury had an undoubted right to form their verdict themselves according to their consciences applying the law to the fact; and if it were otherwise, the first principle of the law of England would be defeated and overthrown.[138]

Burke, during debate in the House of Commons on recent decisions holding that juries had no right to decide the criminality of a libel, said, "Juries ought to take their law from the bench only; but it is our business that they should hear nothing from the bench but what is agreeable to the principles of the constitution."[139] It should be added that Burke thought juries ought to have the right to decide the criminality of the libel, and he was in favor of Parliament insuring this right.[140] This was different from saying that juries had the right to make law. He considered making law the job of Parliament.

So, it is clear that, although the jury did have the right to decide matters of law in the years following the Glorious Revolution of 1688, the right eroded, and thus by the time of the American Revolution the jury in England no longer held this privilege.[141] It would have died altogether except for the agitation which was stirred up in England on the subject of libel. This debate on the right of the jury to decide law, as we will see, spilled into the colonies where it was seldom understood in terms of the origin of the controversy.

The history of the grand jury during this period was not extraordinary, as it suffered, along with the jury, from the existence of the Star Chamber. A statute of 1520, during the reign of Henry VIII, provided for a certificate of justice to be substituted for an indictment in a grand jury action.[142] In the eighteenth century, it was the practice for the grand jury to consist of an odd number of jurors, usually 12 or more. The judge would swear the foreman, and the rest of the jurors swore to abide by that oath insofar as it applied to them. It was punishable for the jurors to disclose the names of those indicted.[143] A peer would not have another trial on oath aside from a grand jury, since he would be tried in the House of Lords where no special oath would be given. In addition, he would not necessarily be tried by his neighbors, but by his peers in the House. In this way it was hoped that the grand jury would have protection from having groundless charges brought against them.[144]

Several special procedures of interest have not yet been mentioned. In 1752, a jury of 12 members could be summoned in cases where only the amount of damages was contested.[145] Another hearing, also seemingly without the presence of a judge, was established for the County of Middlesex for causes not exceeding 40 shillings. Twelve freeholders were summoned to the court, and with the clerk decided the causes in a summary way by majority vote.[146] In an action *De Aetate Prolanda* in 1515 (action by a minor to establish his minority to avoid debt), the age was proved by a jury of 12. The jurors were required to give the reasons for their decision; e.g., they had children of their own about the same age.[147] These jurors were to be at least 42 years old. The procedure was still in use in 1752.[148] Age was not, however, always proved in this way. If the cause was an action to recover a fine by reason of the fact that it had been wrongfully levied on a minor, the question of age was tried by the judges by inspection.[149]

The trial *Per Medietatem Linguae* was of ancient origin. In 1586, during the reign of Elizabeth, it had this form:

> All manner of Inquests and Proofs, which be to be taken or made amongst Aliens and Denizens, be they Merchants or other, as well before the Mayor of the Staple as before any other Justices or Ministers, although the King be party, the one half of the Inquest or Proof shall be of Denizens, and the other Half of Aliens, if so many Aliens and Foreigners be in Town or Place where such Inquest or Proof is to be taken, that be not Parties, nor with the Parties in Contracts,

Pleas or other Quarrels, where of such Inquests or Proofs ought to be taken; and if there be not so many Aliens, then shall be put in such Inquests or Proofs as many Aliens as shall be found in the same Towns or Places, which the Parties as afore is said, and the Remnant of Denizens, which be good men and not suspicious to the one Party nor to the other.[150]

This statute was repealed in the case of treason in 1554. A party entitled to the benefit of the statute had to claim it on the award of the writ of *venire facias* which directed the sheriff to summon the jury. Denizens and aliens were sworn alternately. Denizens, neither aliens nor naturalized citizens, could not be challenged because of the lack of a freehold.[151]

Older modes of trial continued to have some validity. Trial by compurgation was used in the court of the Hundred of Winchester in Sussex in 1440-41,[152] and another example is found in 1699.[153] In 1752, a person could still defend himself against the claim for a debt not evidenced by any writing by swearing that he did not owe the debt and finding 11 of his neighbors who would swear to his honesty.[154] By this time, however, compurgation was seldom used.[155]

Trial by battle continued to be at least a strict legal possibility. In one example, the parties went through the usual preliminaries in 1422. The action concerned a Writ of Right, or an action to recover real estate in which the tenant (defendant) could either elect to put himself upon the Grand Assize, or appeal to battle and the judgment of God. In this example, the tenant chose battle and named his champion. The demandant did likewise. Both champions were commanded to put a penny in each finger stall of their gauntlets. They both appeared in court on the day named, one on either side, bare-headed and kneeling. They then went to separate churches to pray that the outcome of the battle would be just. It is recorded that one went to St. Paul's and the other to Westminster. The battle itself did not occur because the tenant defaulted, as his champion did not appear.[15] There were similar examples in 1571 and 1638.[157]

In 1752, *The Complete Juryman*, in addition to trial by jury, compurgation and battle, also lists trials by record (this includes

former judgments, legality of marriage, bastardy, ex-
communication and the like by certificate of the bishop of the
diocese); customs of London by word of mouth of the recorder
of London; and dower by a justice.[158]

In addition to the Court of Common Pleas and the King's
Bench, there were several other courts during these centuries.
The Court of Equity, for example, became a distinct court in the
fifteenth century.[159] The Admiralty was reorganized under
Henry VII, and even held juries in criminal cases. The use of
juries by this court disappeared when that jurisdiction was
transferred to the common law courts.[160] There were also the
ecclesiastical courts, the Court of the Exchequer (a branch of the
Privy Council), the courts of the hundreds and private courts.[161]
A Court of High Commissioners existed only under the Tudor
monarchs.[162] Justices of the Peace continued to gain in prestige
and importance and, in the 1660's, were the county officials of
most importance.[163]

A description of the trial of Alice Lisle for high treason in
1685 will give some idea of why there was dissatisfaction with
the brand of royal justice to be had under the Restoration
monarchy. The treason Alice Lisle was alleged to have committed was giving shelter to a man named Hicks after he had
been engaged in rebellion against the king. The entire question
depended on whether the defendant knew that Hicks had been
in the rebel army when she had him in her home.

After some deliberation, this dialogue was held between the
foreman of the jury and George Jefferies, Lord Chief Justice of
the King's Bench:

> Foreman: My Lord, we have one thing to beg of your
> lordship, some directions in, before we can give our
> verdict in this case; We have some doubt upon us,
> whether there be sufficient proof that she knew Hicks
> to have been in the army.

> L.C.J. Jefferies: There is as full as proof as proof can
> be, but you are judges of the proof, for my part I
> thought there was no difficulty in it.

Alice Lisle was convicted, attainted and executed.

An Act of Parliament in 1689 declared:

> Whereas Alicia Lisle ... by an irregular and undue
> prosecution, was indicted for entertaining, concealing
> and comforting John Hicks, clerk, a false traitor,
> knowing him to be such, though, the said Hicks was
> not at the trial of the said Alicia Lisle, attainted or con-
> victed of any such crime: and by a verdict injuriously
> exhorted and procured by the menaces and violences
> and other illegal practices of George Lord Jefferies,
> baron of Wren, the Lord Chief Justice of the King's
> Bench ... that it be declared by the authority of Parlia-
> ment ... that the said conviction, judgment and attain-
> ter of the said Alicia be and are hereby repealed...[164]

In the history of the jury, two cases of the greatest importance were the trial of William Penn and William Mead before a
jury at Old Bailey in 1670, and the sequel to the cases, the
Habeas Corpus action on behalf of Edward Bushell, one of the
jurors at the Penn and Mead trial. The first case took place on
September 1, 3, 4 and 5, 1670.[165] The case charged that Penn
and Mead, with about 300 others, on the 10th of August at
11:00 o'clock in the Parish of St. Bennet Grace-Church,

> ...unlawfully and tumultously did assemble and con-
> gregate themselves together, to the disturbance of the
> peace of the said lord the king ... William Penn ... did
> take upon himself to preach and speak ... unto the ...
> persons there assembled....

causing, it was alleged, great terror and disturbance to the
people. Mead was charged with conspiring with Penn to cause
the disturbance.

As the trial commenced, Penn desired a copy of the indictment to read before making his plea. He was told that he
could have it afterwards. Penn and Mead were both fined 40
marks for not having their hats on, although one of the court
attachés had told them to uncover their heads. Bushell, one of
the jurors, had to be sworn again, as it was claimed he had not
kissed the book. During the evidence, which apparently consisted only of crown witnesses, Penn conducted an intelligent

and spirited cross-examination. Mead refused to answer a question of the recorder (judge) on the ground "that no man is bound to accuse himself."

The jury had been retired for an hour and a half when it returned with eight in agreement. At this point, J. Robinson, a member of the bench in the case, had this exchange with Bushell:

> J. Robinson: Mr. Bushell, I have known you near this 14 years; you have thrust yourself upon this jury because you think there is some service for you: I tell you, you deserve to be indicted more than any man that hath been brought to bar this day;

> Bushell: No, Sir John, there were threescore before me, and I would willingly have got off, but could not.

The jury retired for the second time and returned with this verdict, "Guilty of speaking Grace-Church Street." This did not satisfy the court who wanted the words "unlawful assembly" to be included in the verdict. The Recorder said:

> The law of England will not allow you to part till you have given in you verdict.

> Jury: We have given in our verdict and we can give in no other.

The jury asked for and was given pen and ink whereupon they retired again. They soon returned with this written verdict:

> William Penn to be Guilty of speaking or preaching to an assembly, met together in Grace-Church Street, the 14 of August last 1670. And that William Mead is Not Guilty of the said Indictment.

Foreman Thomas Veer and the names of the others were on the verdict, the second being Bushell. The Recorder's reply was,

> Gentlemen, you shall not be dismissed till we have a verdict that the court will accept: and you shall be locked up, without meat, drink, fire, and tobacco; we shall have a verdict, by the help of God, or you shall starve for it.

Penn then addressed the jurors, telling them that he and Mead had used no force of arms but had met outdoors because soldiers had kept them out of their houses. He also said,

> You are Englishmen, mind your privelege, give not away your right.

> Bushell and others: Nor will we ever do it.

One juror now claimed to be indisposed and desired to be dismissed. The mayor, also a part of the bench, said, "You are as strong as any of them; starve them; and hold your principles."

This was on the third of September. It being time for court to close for the day, an observer (probably Penn) described the proceeding:

> The court swore several persons to keep the Jury all night without meat, drink, fire or any other accomodation; they had not so much as a chamberpot, though desired.

The next day the jury returned a verdict finding Mead not guilty and Penn guilty of speaking in Grace-Church Street. The Recorder said he couldn't receive the verdict because the charge included conspiracy and the verdicts were inconsistent. Where-upon, Penn said,

> If Not Guilty be not a verdict, then you make the jury and Magna Carta but a mere nose of wax.

The jury retired again and returned with the same verdict. This was once more turned down by the bench. On their part, the jury refused the suggestion that they return a special verdict. They were remanded to Newgate for the night. The following day, the fifth, the jury returned a verdict of not guilty as to both parties. It appears that the jury had been without food and drink in excess of two days.

The Recorder fined the jury 40 marks each (a little over 26 pounds) and sent them to jail until it was paid. Penn was fined for contempt. He protested, citing passages of the Magna Carta. Penn also had the last word, saying later, "Magna Charta is Magna f____with the Recorder of London; and to demand right and affront to the court."

Bushell, on his part, didn't take the fine lying down. He obtained a writ of Habeas Corpus.[166] The opinion was written on November 20th of the same year by Chief Justice Baughan, and never after were juries to be punished for not finding in accordance with the court's instructions. The moment is marked for posterity by a plaque hanging in Old Bailey and inscribed as follows:

Near this Site
WILLAM PENN and WILLIAM MEAD
were tried in 1670
for preaching to an unlawful assembly
in Grace-Church Street
This tablet Commemorates
The courage and endurance of the Jury Thos Vere, Edward Bushell and ten others who refused to give a Verdict against them, although locked up without food for two nights and were fined for their final Verdict of Not Guilty.

The case of these Jurymen was reviewed on a Writ of Habeas Corpus and Chief Justice Vaughan delivered the opinion of the Court which established 'The Right of Juries' to give their Verdict according to their Convictions.

Because of these jurors and this decision, the jury deserved the high position it held in the esteem of Englishmen. In time to come, the jury was to lose much of its vitality in the country that had nurtured it. The Englishmen, however, who were at that very time settling the American colonies, carried with them from the earliest times the jury as a guarantee of liberty. On that continent, the jury was to gain new life and new meaning.

Chapter VI Footnotes

1. *The Security of Englishmen's Lives*, Lord Somers (London, 1766 Ed., reprint of 1681), p. 102.

2. *History of Trial By Jury*, William Forsyth (John W. Parker and Son, London, 1852), pp. 96-97.

3. *A Preliminary Treatise on Evidence,* James Bradley Thayer (Sweet and Maxwell, London, 1898), p. 75.

4. *Id.* at p. 76.

5. "Early Opposition to the Petty Jury In Criminal Cases," Charles L. Wells, 30 Law Q. Rev. 97, at 104.

6. Thayer, *op. cit.* at note 3, at p. 76.

7. Wells, *op. cit.* at note 5, at p. 104.

8. The Proof of Guilt, Glanville Williams (Stevens and Sons, London, 1963 ed., 1st printed 1955), p. 13.

9. *The Complete Juryman,* anonymous (London, 1752), pp. 162-63.

10. *Id.* at p. 35.

11. *The Complete Juryman, op. cit.* at note 9, at p. 36.

12. *A History of English Law,* Sir William Holdsworth (Sweet and Maxwell Ltd., London, 7th Ed. 1956, 1st Ed. 1903), I-332.

13. Thayer, *op. cit.* at note 3, at p. 91.

14. *A Guide To English Juries,* by a person of quality (Attr. by Forsyth to Lord Somers) (London, 1682), p. 5.

15. *The Complete Juryman, op. cit.* at note 9, at pp. 26, 27.

16. *The Statutes at Large,* I William and Mary, Sess. 2.C2. 1698 (Cambridge, 1762), Vol. I.

17. *The Complete Juryman, op. cit.* at note 9, at p. 11.

18. *The Complete Juryman, op. cit.* at note 9, at p. 5 of preface.

19. *The Complete Juryman, op. cit.* at note 9, at p. 79.

20. *The Complete Juryman, op. cit.* at note 9, at pp. 37-40.

21. *A Guide To English Juries, op. cit.* at note 14, at p. 7.

22. *The Complete Juryman, op. cit.* at note 9, at pp. 107-10.

23. *The Complete Juryman, op. cit.* at note 9, at pp. 128-30.

24. Holdsworth, *op. cit.* at note 12, at I-336.

25. *The Complete Juryman, op. cit.* at note 9, at p. 114.

26. *The Complete Juryman, op. cit.* at note 9, at pp. 31-33.

27. *The Complete Juryman, op. cit.* at note 9, at pp. 135-38.

28. *The Complete Juryman, op. cit.* at note 9, at pp. 128-30, 133.

29. *Plumpton Correspondence,* Thomas Stapleton, editor (John Bowyer Nichols and Son, London, 1839), p. 134.

30. *The Complete Juryman, op. cit.* at note 9, at p. 151.

31. *The Complete Juryman, op. cit.* at note 9, at pp. 73-75.

32. Thayer, *op. cit.* at note 3, at p. 92.

33. Thayer, *op. cit.* at note 3, at p. 92.

34. *Plumpton Correspondence, op. cit.* at note 29, at p. 159.

35. *Plumpton Correspondence, op. cit.* at note 29, at p. 134.

36. *A Guide To English Juries, op. cit.* at note 14, at p. 202.

37. *History of Trial By Jury,* William Forsyth (John Parker and Son, London, 1852), p. 172.

38. *Id.* at p. 176.

39. "Trial By Juror and the Reform of Civil Procedure," Austin Wakeman, 31 Harv. L. Rev. 669 (1918), at p. 677.

40. *History of the English Law,* John Reeves (Reed and Hunter, London, 1814), IV-195.

41. *The Complete Juryman, op. cit.* at note 9, at p. 122.

42. *The Complete Juryman, op. cit.* at note 9, at p. 171.

43. *The Complete Juryman, op. cit.* at note 9, at p. 170.

44. *The Complete Juryman, op. cit.* at note 9, at p. 171.

45. *Ibid.,* and *Trial by Jury,* Sir Patrick Devlin (Stevens and Sons, London, 3rd Ed. 1966, 1st printed 1956), p. 50.

46. Williams, *op. cit.* at note 8, at p. 6.

47. Somers, *op. cit.* at note 1, at p. 103.

48. *A Guide to English Juries, op. cit.* at note 14, at p. 103.

49. *The Complete Juryman, op. cit.* at note 9, at p. 4.

50. *The Jury,* W.R. Cornish (Penguin Press, London, 1968), p. 70.

51. Williams, *op. cit.* at note 8, at p. 11.

52. Williams, *op. cit.* at note 8, at p. 73.

53. *The Complete Juryman, op. cit.* at note 9, at p. 206.

54. Williams, *op. cit.* at note 8, at p. 70.

55. Wells, *op. cit.* at note 5, at p. 108.

56. *Ibid.*

57. Williams, *op. cit.* at note 8, at p. 6.

58. Wells, *op. cit.* at note 5, at p. 108.

59. Cornish, *op. cit.* at note 52, at p. 72; Wells, *op. cit.* at note 5, at p. 108, citing cases in 1565 and 1590 where only crown witnesses presented.

60. Williams, *op. cit.* at note 8, at p. 70.

61. Holdsworth, *op. cit.* at note 12, at I-325-26.

62. *State Trials,* T.B. Howell, editor (T.C. Hansard, London, 1816), Vol. I, p. xxix of the preface.

63. Forsyth, *op. cit.* at note 37, at p. 161.

64. Holdsworth, *op. cit.* at note 12, at I-335.

65. *Ibid.*

66. Thayer, *op. cit.* at note 3, at p. 125.

67. Holdsworth, *op. cit.* at note 12, at I-335.

68. Williams, *op. cit.* at note 8, at p. 206.

69. Holdsworth, *op. cit.* at note 12, at I-319, 343.

70. Wakeman, *op. cit.* at note 39, at p. 680.

71. Thayer, *op. cit.* at note 3, at p. 211.

72. *A Guide to English Juries, op. cit.* at note 14, at p. 38.

73. *Id.* at p. 125.

74. Cornish, *op. cit.* at note 52, at pp. 32-33.

75. *The Complete Juryman, op. cit.* at note 9, at pp. 66, 68.

76. Thayer, *op. cit.* at note 3, at p. 94.

77. Thayer, *op. cit.* at note 3, at p. 96.

78. *The Complete Juryman, op. cit.* at note 9, at p. 5 of preface and p. 66.

79. *The Complete Juryman, op. cit.* at note 9, at p. 175.

80. *The Complete Juryman, op. cit.* at note 9, at p. 176.

81. *The Complete Juryman, op. cit.* at note 9, at pp. 174, 194.

82. Forsyth, *op. cit.* at note 37, at p. 185.

83. Thayer, *op. cit.* at note 3, at p. 162.

84. *Ibid.*

85. Reeves, *op. cit.* at note 42, at IV-195.

86. Cornish, *op. cit.* at note 52, at p. 128.

87. Thayer, *op. cit.* at note 3, at p. 164.

88. Thayer, *op. cit.* at note 3, at pp. 164-66.

89. *State Trials, op. cit.* at note 40, at VI-995.

90. Williams, *op. cit.* at note 8, at p. 257.

91. Holdsworth, *op. cit.* at note 12, at I-343-44.

92. *The Englishman's Right,* Sir John Hawles (6th ed., London, 1771, reprint of 1680 ed.), p. 31.

93. *The Complete Juryman, op. cit.* at note 9, at p. 205.

94. *A History of Lay Judges,* John P. Dawson (Harvard Univ. Press, Cambridge, Mass, 1960), p. 172.

95. *An Enquiry Into the Doctrine Lately Propagated Concerning Libels, Warrants and the Seizure of Papers,* Father of Candor (Burlington House, London, 1764), p. 5.

96. Williams, *op. cit.* at note 8, at p. 402.

97. Holdsworth, *op. cit.* at note 12, at pp. I-343-44.

98. Forsyth, *op. cit.* at note 37, at p. 185.

99. Thayer, *op. cit.* at note 3, at pp. 162-63.

100. *The Works and Correspondence of Edmund Burke,* Charles William, editor (Francis and John Rivington, London, 1852 ed., 1st ed. 1844), IV-140.

101. Thayer, *op. cit.* at note 3, at p. 101.

102. Thayer, *op. cit.* at note 3, at p. 102.

103. Devlin, *op. cit.* at note 47, at pp. 69, 70.

104. Thayer, *op. cit.* at note 3 at pp. 111, 174.

105. *The Complete Juryman, op. cit.* at note 9, at p. 177.

106. *State Trials, op. cit.* at note 40, at VII-259.

107. Thayer, *op. cit.* at note 3, at p. 174.

108. *The Origin of Juries,* Heinrich Brunner (Berlin, 1872), p. 437.

109. Thayer, *op. cit.* at note 3, at p. 104.

110. *Commentaries on the Laws of England,* William Blackstone (7th Ed., Oxford, 1775, 1st ed. 1665), III-367.

111. *The Complete Juryman, op. cit.* at note 9, at p. 262.

112. *Plumpton Correspondence, op. cit.* at note 29, at p. 141.

113. Wakeman, *op. cit.* at note 39, at p. 681; Forsyth, *op. cit.* at note 37, at p. 161; Thayer, *op. cit.* at note 3, at p. 170.

114. Thayer, *op. cit.* at note 3, at p. 172.

115. Forsyth, *op. cit.* at note 37, at pp. 188-91.

116. Thayer, *op. cit.* at note 3, at p. 175.

117. Thayer, *op. cit.* at note 3, at p. 177.

118. *Ibid.*

119. Thayer, *op. cit.* at note 3, at p. 178.

120. *The Complete Juryman, op. cit.* at note 9, at p. 166.

121. *The Complete Juryman, op. cit.* at note 9, at p. 164.

122. *The Complete Juryman, op. cit.* at note 9, at pp. 154-59.

123. *The Complete Juryman, op. cit.* at note 9, at pp. 159-61.

124. *Plumpton Correspondence, op. cit.* at note 29, at p. 141.

125. *The Complete Juryman, op. cit.* at note 9, at p. 23.

126. Thayer, *op. cit.* at note 3, at pp. 151-52.

127. Thayer, *op. cit.* at note 3, at p. 154.

128. *A Guide to English Juries, op. cit.* at note 14, at pp. 29-30.

129. Holdsworth, *op. cit.* at note 12, at I-342.

130. Somers, *op. cit.* at note 1, at p. 11.

131. Hawles, *op. cit.* at note 92, at p. 14.

132. Hawles, *op. cit.* at note 92, at p. 11.

133. *Reports of Cases Argued and Adjudged in the Superior Court of Judicature of the Province of Massachusetts Bay Between 1761-1772,* Josiah Quincy, Jr., editor (Little, Brown, and Company, Boston, 1865), p. 561.

134. *Ibid.*

135. *The Complete Juryman, op. cit.* at note 9, at p. 2.

136. *The Complete Juryman, op. cit.* at note 9, at p. 246.

137. *An Enquiry into the Use and Practice of Juries Among the Greeks and Romans,* John Pettingal (London, 1769), pp. 121-22.

138. Quincy, *op. cit.* at note 133, at p. 562.

139. Williams, *op. cit.* at note 100, at IV-145.

140. Williams, *op. cit.* at note 100, at IV-138-46.

141. Quincy, *op. cit.* at note 133, at p. 562; Wakeman, *op. cit.* at note 39, at p. 677.

142. Pettingal, *op. cit.* at note 137, at p. 35.

143. *The Complete Juryman, op. cit.* at note 9, at pp. 12,18.

144. *A Guide to Juries, op. cit.* at note 14, at p. 60.

145. *The Complete Juryman, op. cit.* at note 9, at p. 3.

146. *Capital Traction* v. *Hof,* 174 U.S. 1 (1898), at p. 17.

147. Thayer, *op. cit.* at note 3, at p. 20.

148. *The Complete Juryman, op. cit.* at note 9, at p. 36.

149. *The Complete Juryman, op. cit.* at note 9, at p. 278.

150. *The Complete Juryman, op. cit.* at note 9, at p. 146.

151. *The Complete Juryman, op. cit.* at note 9, at pp. 23, 148, 165.

152. Thayer, *op. cit.* at note 3, at p. 26.

153. Thayer, *op. cit.* at note 3, at p. 31.

154. *The Complete Juryman, op. cit.* at note 9, at p. 281.

155. Thayer, *op. cit.* at note 3, at p. 32.

156. *The Complete Juryman, op. cit.* at note 9, at pp. 283-84.

157. Thayer, *op. cit.* at note 3, at p. 43.

158. *The Complete Juryman, op. cit.* at note 9, at pp. 278-82.

159. Dawson, *op. cit.* at note 94, at p. 149.

160. Dawson, *op. cit.* at note 94, at p. 174.

161. Dawson, *op. cit.* at note 94, at pp. 174, 182.

162. Dawson, *op. cit.* at note 94, at p. 174.

163. Dawson, *op. cit.* at note 94, at p. 297.

164. *State Trials, op. cit.* at note 40, at XI-298-307.

165. *State Trials, op. cti.* at note 40, at VI-951-969.

166. *State Trials, op. cit.* at note 40, at VI-999-1111.

VII

The Jury in America to 1800

When Englishmen first came to North America, they brought trial by jury with them. The First Charter of Virginia (1606) provided that all subjects in the colonies should,

> ...have and enjoy all Liberties, Franchises, and Immunities within any of our Dominions, to all Intents and Purposes, as if they had been abidding and born, within this our realm of England, or any other of our said Dominions.[1]

The right to trial by jury was specifically mentioned in King James I's Instructions for the Government of the Colony of Virginia, on November 20, 1606. Minor offenses, such as drunkenness and idleness were not tried by a jury. All capital crimes, which included major disturbances, rebellion, conspiracy, sedition, murder, manslaughter, incest, rape, and adultery, were to be tried by juries.[2]

Trial by jury was introduced into the Massachusetts Bay Colony by 1628.[3] The Massachusetts Body of Liberties, adopted by the General Court of Massachusetts on December 10, 1641, contains detailed and unusual provisions concerning trial by jury. The following are those provisions:

> Art. 29 — In all actions at law it shall be the libertee of the plaintife and defendant by mutual consent to choose whether they will be tryed by the Bench or by a Jurie, unless it be where the law upon just reason hath otherwise determined. The like libertie shall be granted to all persons in criminall cases.

> Art. 30 — It shall be in libertie both of Plaintife and defendant, and likewise every delinquent (to be judged by a Jurie) to challenge any of the Jurors and if his challenge be found just and reasonable by the Bench, or the rest of the Jurie, as the challenger shall choose,

it shall be allowed him. And tales de cercumstantibus impaneled in their room.

Art. 31 — In all cases where evidence is so obscure or defective that the Jurie cannot clearly and safely give a positive verdict, whether it be a grand or petit Jurie, It shall have libertie to give a nonLiquit, or a spetiall verdict, in which last, that is in a spetiall verdict, the Judgment of the cause shall be left to the Court, and all Jurors shall have libertie in matters of fact if they cannot finde the maine issue, yet to find and present in their verdict so much as they can, If the Bench and Jurors shall so differ at any time about their verdict that either of them cannot proceede with peace of conscience the case shall be referred to the General Court, who shall take the question from both and determine it.

Article 57 provided for the summoning of a jury of 12 freemen to inquire into the cause of death. Article 49 limited jury service to two courts a year, except grand jurors were required to hold at least two courts a year. The jurors, pursuant to Article 50, were chosen by the freemen of the town where they lived. Finally, there were these two interesting provisions:

Art. 76 — Whensoever any Jurie of trialls or Jurors are not cleare in their Judgments or conscience conserning any cause wherein they are to give their verdict, they shall have libertie in open Court to advise with any man they think fitt to resolve or direct them before they give in their verdict.

Art. 77 — In all cases wherein any freeman is to give his vote, be it in point of Election, making constitutions and orders, or passing sentence in any case of Judicature or the like, if he cannot see reason to give it positively one way or an other, he shall have libertie to be silent, and not be pressed to a determined vote.[4]

The Concessions and Agreements of West New Jersey (1677) contained the following guarantee of trial by jury:

Chp. XVII — That no Proprietor, freeholder or inhabitant of the said Province of West New Jersey, shall be deprived or condemned of life, limb, liberty, estate, property or any ways hurt in his or their privileges, freedoms or franchises, upon any account whatsoever, without a due tryal, and judgment passed by twelve, good and lawful men of his neighbourhood first had: and that in all causes to be tryed, and in all tryals, the person or persons, arraigned may except against any of the said neighbourhood, without any reason rendered, (not exceeding thirty-five) and in case of any valid reason alleged, against every person nominated for that service.[5]

When the English occupied New Amsterdam in 1664 and renamed it New York, they again brought the jury with them. In early cases on Long Island, an appeal was permitted from a jury verdict to a court of equity.[6] Jury trials were held in Pennsylvania under the Duke as early as 1673, and in that year, county courts were instituted with juries of six or seven, where a majority could render a verdict.[7] The Frame of Government of Pennsylvania (1682), the year after William Penn was made proprietor of the colony, contained this provision:

VIII. That all trials shall be by twelve men, and as near as may be, peers or equals, and of the neighbourhood, and men without just exception; in cases of life, there shall be first twenty-four returned by the Sheriffs, for a grand inquest, of whom twelve, at least, shall find the complaint to be true; and then the twelve men, or peers, to be likewise returned by the sheriff, shall have the final judgment. But reasonable challenges shall be always admitted against the said twelve men, or any of them.[8]

In early Connecticut, upon the continual failure of the jurors to agree, the verdict could be decided by a majority vote; if it was a tie, the magistrate presiding cast the deciding vote.[9] By at least 1693, a jury could be waived in misdemeanor cases in Baltimore,[10] and even admiralty cases were tried by juries in some states.[11] During colonial times, trial judges were generally unpopular, incompetent and without legal training.[12] It may be by reason of these considerations that their powers at trial were limited in both civil and criminal cases.[13] Lawyers were also as unpopular as judges. Chapter XXII of the Concessions and Agreements of West New Jersey provided that, "...no person or persons shall be compelled to fee any attorney or counciller to plead his cause, but all persons have free liberty to plead his own cause, if he please...."[14] It is reasoned that the absence of lawyers made impossible a highly developed system of law.[15]

Trial by jury had its setbacks during colonial times. It was not adopted initially in New Haven.[16] After the early settlement of Virginia, the jury system had been restrained by laws contrary to the common law of England, although this problem was corrected by legislation in 1661-62.[17] During the late colonial period, British procedures did not provide for jury trial for crimes relating to liquor, labor, smuggling and assaults.[18]

The charge of attaint was a problem to jurors in America as it was in England, and was used, for example, in Rhode Island.[19] The Massachusetts General Court passed an act requiring every verdict of a jury to be accepted unless the party which lost attainted the jury, whereupon the court would impanel a jury of 24 upon whose verdict final judgment was rendered.[20] This remedy became so popular by 1684 that another statute was passed providing that if the person bringing the attaint lost, he would be fined 34 pounds and the jury against which the attaint was brought could prosecute him for slander.[21] The remedy became less popular.[22] Alexander Hamilton, in *The Federalist*, makes reference to appeals from one jury to another in Georgia and in Rhode Island, Connecticut, New Hampshire and Massachusetts, until one party had two verdicts.[23] He was probably referring to attaint. By Hamilton's time, the remedy was nearly as obsolete in the colonies as in England.[24]

As in England, the practice of ordering a new trial in civil cases when the trial judge disagreed with the verdict made attaint unnecessary. When the order was made by a court of appeal, the order for a new trial was called a *venire facias de novo*.[25] Special verdicts were used as early as 1657 in Massachusetts,[26] and a number of examples of new trials are reported for Pennsylvania for the 1760's.[27]

For minor crimes, conviction and punishment could be had without a jury. Punishment by whipping (up to 10 strokes), the stocks (up to three hours), the ducking stool, and fines and imprisonment could all be imposed by magistrates in Massachusetts without a jury. If, however, bond was posted, a jury could be had on appeal.[28]

The importance of jury trial to the colonists and early citizens of the newly formed American republic is proved by the frequency to which it was referred in their revolutionary and constitutional documents. The Declaration of Rights of the First Continental Congress, issued on October 14, 1774, included this passage:

> ...the respective colonies are entitled to the common law of England, and more especially to the great and inestimable privilege of being tried by their peers of the vincinage according to the course of law.[29]

On October 19, 1775, The First Session of the American Stamp Act Congress issued resolutions considered to contain "...the most essential rights and liberties of the colonists...," among which was the clause, "That trial by jury is the inherent and invaluable right of every British subject in these Colonies."[30] Nine of the thirteen colonies supported this principle,[31] and, in fact, it became an increasingly influential argument in the debate against English rule. On July 6, 1775, as one of the reasons for taking up arms, it was claimed that the colonists had been deprived "...of the accustomed and inestimable privilege of trial by jury, in cases affecting both life and property." This statement was contained in the "Declaration of the Causes and Necessity of Taking Up Arms."[32]

The Constitution of Virginia was published on June 12 and adopted June 29, 1776, and can be considered the first written constitution of a modern republican government. These guarantees of trial by jury were contained in Virginia's Bill of Rights:

> Sec. 8. That in all capital or criminal prosecutions a man has a right ... to a speedy trial by an impartial jury of twelve men of his vincinage, without whose unanimous consent he cannot be found guilty, ... that

no man be deprived of his liberty, except by the law of
the land or the judgment of his peers.

Sec. 11. That in controversies respecting property, and
in suits between man and man, the ancient trial by
jury is preferable to any other, and ought to be held
sacred.[33]

The reference to "judgment of his peers" was a clear reference
to the Magna Carta, which, regardless of the scholars, is still regarded as the original guarantee of the jury trial. Section 11 of
the charter was in fact a specific guarantee of jury trial in civil
cases, and the lack of such a guarantee was one of Thomas Jefferson's objections to the United States Constitution before the
Bill of Rights was passed.[34]

The Declaration of Independence, on the matter of jury
trial, was brief but to the point, declaring that one of the reasons necessitating the separation of the colonies from England
was, "For depriving us, in many cases, of the benefits of Trial by
Jury."[35] The Articles of Confederation, drafted in 1777, contained no provision establishing a judiciary system,[36] but when
the Continental Congress did have an opportunity to establish a
system of trial, it provided for trial by jury. The Ordinance For
the Government of the Territory of the United States Northwest of the Ohio River was passed on July 13, 1787 and revived
under the new Constitution, dated August 7, 1799. It provided:

Art. 11 — The inhabitants of the said territory shall be
entitled to the benefits of the writs of habeas corpus
and of the trial by jury... No man shall be deprived of
his liberty or propery, but by the judgment of his
peers, or the law of the land....[37]

For the most part, the states were quicker to incorporate
the right to trial by jury into formal documents. Pennsylvania,
on August 16, 1776, adopted provisions relative to jury trial
which were very nearly identical to those contained in the constitution of Virginia.[38] The provision adopted by Delaware in
September of the same year was also much the same as Virginia's guarantee of jury trial in criminal cases.[39] On November
3, 1776, Maryland adopted the following constitutional provi-

sions guaranteeing trial by jury:

> III. That the inhabitants of Maryland are entitled to the common law of England and the trial by jury...
>
> XIX. That in all criminal prosecutions, every man hath a right to ... a speedy trial by an impartial jury, without whose unanimous consent he ought not to be found guilty.
>
> XXI. ...or deprived of his life, liberty or property, but by the judgment of his peers, or by the law of the land.[40]

On December 14, 1776, the constitution of North Carolina achieved much the same objectives with substantially different language:

> IX. That no freeman shall be convicted of any crime but by the unanimous verdict of a jury of good and lawful men, in open court as heretofore used.
>
> XIV. That in all controversies at law, respecting property, the ancient mode of trial, by jury, is one of the best securities of the rights of the people, and ought to remain sacred and inviolate.[41]

The word "freeman" was no doubt a reference to the institution of slavery as it existed in America, but it is also reminiscent of the language of the Magna Carta and the dual status with regard to the condition of freedom that also existed in England at that early time.

Vermont, on July 8, 1777, adopted constitutional provisions insuring trial by jury in both criminal and civil causes much like those adopted by Virginia.[42] In the same year, Georgia adopted constitutional provisions guaranteeing trial by jury with this addition: "...the jury shall be judges of law, as well as fact, and shall not be allowed to bring in a special verdict."[43]

Massachusetts adopted its constitution on October 25, 1780, and guaranteed trial by jury in language differing from the rest:

XII. ...And no subject shall be arrested, imprisoned, despoiled or
     deprived his property, immunities, or privileges, put out of
     the protection of the law, exiled, or deprived of his life,
     liberty, or estate, but by the judgment of his peers or the
     law of the land.

     And the legislature shall not make any law that shall
     subject any person to a capital or infamous punishment,
     excepting for the government of the army or navy, with-
     out trial by Jury.

XV. In all controversies concerning property, and in all
     suits between two or more persons, except in cases in
     which it has heretofore been otherways used and prac-
     ticed, the parties have a right to a trial by jury; and this
     method of procedure shall be held sacred, unless, in causes
     arising on the high seas, and such as relate to mariners'
     wages, the legislature hereafter find it necessary to alter
     it.[44]

This constitution, while substantially similar to the language of
Article 39 of the Magna Carta, seems concerned that the protection not be too broad, hence the exceptions for the military, past
practice and mariners' wages. Of the models available in 1784,
New Hampshire chose to substantially adopt Massachusetts'
jury guarantees.[45]

Connecticut, despite its lack of actual constitutional provisions for trial by jury, made perhaps more use of the jury than
many of the other states because they didn't have distinct courts
of chancery and admiralty.[46] Rhode Island, on the other hand,
did not adopt a constitution until 1843, but continued under the
Colonial Charter of 1663.[47]

The effort to preserve the jury in a pure form is highlighted
by a case decided by the Supreme Court of New Jersey in the
year 1780. The legislature had passed a statute providing for a
jury of six. The court held this provision unconstitutional, saying, "...the inestimable right of trial by jury shall remain confirmed as part of the law of this colony without repeal forever."
This was the first piece of legislation to be held unconstitutional
in the United States.[48]

When the Federal Constitution became effective on March 4, 1789, it contained this provision guaranteeing trial by jury in criminal cases:

> Art. 3, Sec. 3 — The Trial of all Crimes, except in cases of Impeachment, shall be by Jury; and such Trial shall be held in the State where the said Crime shall have been committed; but when not committed within any State, the Trial shall be at such place or places as the Congress may by Law have enacted.[49]

This laconic provision was deemed insufficient, as it was objected that it contained no provision for the trial of civil cases by the jury. This prompted Alexander Hamilton to devote number 83 of the *Federalist* papers to this subject. He observed:

> The objection to the plan of the convention, which has met with most success in this State, and perhaps in several of the other States, is *that relative to the want of a constitutional provision* for the trial by jury in civil cases. [Emphasis Hamilton's][50]

He was quick to note that all concerned valued the jury:

> The friends and adversaries of the plan of the convention, if they agree in nothing else, concur at least in the value they set upon the trial by jury; or if there is any difference between them if consists in this: the former regard it as a valuable safeguard to liberty; the latter represent it as the palladium of free government.[51]

Hamilton's own view held the criminal jury in "high estimation",[52] but he could not. "...readily discern the inseparable connection between the existence of liberty, and the trial by jury in civil cases".[53]

While the opponents did not defeat the adoption of the Constitution, they did succeed in having it amended to insure the preservation of the right to trial by jury. They were so successful in this respect that when the Bill of Rights was sent to the legislature of the states for ratification, no less than three out of 10 of the proposed amendments contained guarantees of various aspects of trial by jury:

> Amendment V — No person shall be held to answer
> for a capital, or otherwise infamous crime, unless on a
> presentment or indictment of a Grand Jury, except in
> cases arising in the land or naval forces, or in the Mi-
> litia, when in actual service in time of War or public
> danger;....

> Amendment VI — In all criminal prosecutions the ac-
> cused shall enjoy the right to a speedy and public trial,
> by an impartial jury of the State and district wherein
> the crime shall have been committed, which district
> shall have been previously ascertained by law, and to
> be informed of the nature and cause of the accusation;
> to be confronted with the witnesses against him; to
> have compulsory process for obtaining witnesses in his
> favor, and to have the assistance of Counsel for his de-
> fense....

> Amendment VII — In suits at common law, where the
> value in controversy shall exceed twenty dollars, the
> right of trial by jury shall be preserved, and no fact
> tried by a jury shall be otherwise re-examined in any
> court of the United States, than according to the rules
> of the common law.

In the Penn-Mead trial, previously discussed in the last
chapter, the defendants were not clearly informed of the nature
of the charge before their plea was taken, they were not permitted to call witnesses, and they were not permitted counsel
for their defense. Counsel for the defense did not have a full
right of participation even in England at this time, although they
were allowed to cross-examine witnesses of the crown. Counsel
could not address the jury in criminal cases, although in "all
criminal prosecutions" the defendant was to have a right to trial
by jury. No doubt, latent memories of the Star Chamber suggested the provision regarding grand juries. The jury trial guaranteed in the Bill of Rights was therefore something more than
the right enjoyed by Englishmen in 1791.

It was seen in the last chapter how juries had obtained the

right to decide law as well as facts after the Glorious Revolution of 1688 and how that privilege had been lost by the middle of the eighteenth century. At the time of the American Revolution, the juries in the colonies generally had the prerogative to decide law and fact in civil as well as in criminal cases. In cases decided in 1692, 1764, 1767 and 1773 in Pennsylvania, it was held that the jurors had this right.[54] In a case in Pennsylvania in 1784, opposing counsel argued different law and the jury was charged to make up its own mind as to which was correct.[55] There was only one judge in the United States who, between 1776 and 1800, was to deny the jury the right to decide law in criminal cases. This judge presided in a court of common pleas in Pennsylvania and made this ruling in 1793 in the case of *Pennsylvania* v. *Bell*. He was afterwards impeached by the House of Representatives of Pennsylvania and removed by the Pennsylvania Senate, on the grounds of interference with the rights a fellow judge in the charging of grand and petit juries.[56] The judge was also disqualified to hold any judicial office in the state. By constitutional provision, Pennsylvania provided in 1790 that, "...in all indictments for libels the jury shall have a right to determine the law and the facts under the direction of the court, as in other cases."[57] The words "as in other cases" must have been attached to make sure the provision was not taken to imply the absence of the right in non-libel cases. This is an example of the concern which libel cases stirred up.

New York juries also had the right to decide law in criminal cases between 1776 and 1800, although their right was not clear in civil cases, as the New York Court of Appeals was divided on this question in 1804.[58] The trial of John Peter Zenger for libel in 1735 gives some idea of how the colonial juries came by the right to decide law.[59] Zenger, a printer, had accused the governor of New York with maladministration, corruption and taking the right of trial by jury from the citizens. The preliminaries included a dispute over the jurors' qualifications; however, forty-eight freeholders were chosen and Zenger was permitted to strike 12 of them. Finally, the twelve remaining jurors were chosen for the trial. By this time, Zenger was represented by

Andrew Hamilton of Philadlephia. The words and the publication in question were admitted. Counsel for the crown thought
nothing remained but for the jury to return a verdict for the
king, but Hamilton argued that he should be permitted to prove
the truth of the charges made by Zenger, and in the event his
proof was accepted, the words would not be held libelous.

Hamilton's position drew the comment from the presiding
Chief Justice, "You cannot be admitted, Mr. Hamilton, to give
the truth of a libel in evidence. A libel is not to be justified; for it
is nevertheless a libel that it is true."

The judge was clear that this point of the law was for him
and not for the jury to decide. Hamilton, however, was determined to win his case, and thus immediately addressed the jury:

> I thank your honour. Then gentlemen of the jury,
> it is to you we must now appeal, for witnesses to the
> truth of the facts we have offered and are denied the
> liberty to prove.... The law supposes you to be sum-
> moned out of the neighborhood where the fact is al-
> leged to be committed; and the reason of your being
> taken out of the neighbourhood is because you are
> supposed to have the best knowledge of the fact that is
> to be tried. ...That the suppressing of evidence ought
> always to be taken for the strongest evidence...

The Chief Justice could not be blamed for thinking he had
not made his position clear. He interrupted:

> No, Mr. Hamilton; the jury may find that Mr.
> Zenger printed and published those papers, and leave
> it to the court to judge whether they are libelous. You
> know this is very common; it is in the nature of a spe-
> cial verdict, where the jury leave the matter of law to
> the Court.

Hamilton replied:

> I know, may it please your honour, they may do
> so; but I do likewise know they may do otherwise. I
> know they have the right, beyond all dispute, to deter-
> mine both the law and the fact, and where they have
> no doubt of the law, they ought to do so....

He continued to the jury:

> Gentlemen, the danger is great, in proportion to the mischief that may happen through our too great credulity. A proper confidence in a court is comendable; but the verdict (whatever it is) will be yours, you ought to refer no part of your duty to the discretion of these persons. If you should be of opinion that there is no falsehood in Mr. Zenger's papers, you will, nay (pardon me for the expression) you ought to say so.... It is the best cause; it is the cause of liberty....

The Chief Justice charged the jury:

> Gentlemen of the jury, the great pains Mr. Hamilton has taken to shew how little regard juries are to pay to the opinion of the judges, and his insisting so much upon the conduct of some judges in trials of this kind, is done, no doubt, with a design that you should take but very little notice of what I may say upon this occasion. I shall therefore only observe to you that, as the facts or words in the information are confessed, the only thing that can come in question before you is whether the words, as set forth in the information, make a libel, and that as a matter of law, no doubt, and which you may leave to the court...

The jury was out a short time and returned with a verdict of not guilty, and this result was greeted by cheers from a large crowd. Andrew Hamilton was given the freedom of New York City together with a gold box engraved with a seal of this freedom.[60]

At no time during the trial did the judge concede the right of the jury to decide law, nor did he stop Hamilton from arguing the question to the jury. No doubt the great leeway given to juries after the Glorious Revolution was grounds for the restraint of the court. However, this conduct by counsel would not have been condoned in England, where the accused's counsel was still not permitted to address the jury. The colonies were molding their own idea of jury trial.

Massachusetts jurors were allowed the right to decide law

in a case of 1641, although it was successively repealed and re-granted by enactments in 1642, 1657 and 1660.⁶¹ One of the reasons why Massachusetts jurors were allowed this privilege could be found in the oath incorporated in their jury instructions, cautioning them to deliver their verdict "...according to law and the evidence given you." English jurors on the other hand, were sworn to give their verdict "...according to the evidence." The oath of the Massachusetts jurors was affirmed by the King in 1724.⁶²

If there was sometimes doubt in theory that juries had the right to decide law, there was no doubt in practice. In 1761, a case, *Erving* v. *Cradock,* was brought for trespass against a custom house officer for the detaining of a Brigantine and its cargo. The defendant, in the lower court, pleaded the general issue and the plaintiff obtained judgment. The defendant appealed and the question was submitted to a jury which found in favor of the plaintiff in the amount of 740 pounds.

In a letter to the Lords of Trade, Governor Bernard wrote:

> The whole Bench directed the jury, as strongly as they could, to find for the defendant. Nevertheless they found for the plaintiff and gave upwards of 550 pounds sterling in damages, being all he said he was out of pocket. This was no surprise to those that were acquainted with the violence with which there proceedings are carried on. It was remarkable that Mr. Erving according to the Usage of there courts, spoke a great deal for himself, when he had admitted everything necessary to prove that he had incurred a forfeiture and declared he acquiesced only in expectation that a time should come when he should have his *revenge;* a word he used several times to express the purpose of his conduct.... A custom house officer has no chance with a jury, let his cause be what it will.

The case was appealed, and the plaintiff, on February 27, 1762, signed a satisfaction of judgment in order that the matter would be moot, and he could therefore avoid answering the appeal.⁶³ In this case, as in the Zenger case, it was not so much a matter of the court recognizing the jury's right to decide law, but deferring to their decision of it. In other words, if the jury had held a prerogative actually enforceable by the courts, then the appeal would have been no threat to the verdict. Present day counsel will sympathize with Erving's lawyer for having a client who took so much on himself.

This was not an isolated case. *Goodspeed* v. *Gay* (1763) was an action of trover against a military officer who allegedly recruited the plaintiff's slave. The plaintiff gained the verdict. Again we have Governor Bernard's comment, "...upon tryal the Judges told the jury that there was no evidence against the defendant, not the least pretence to charge him in such an action."[64]

Both of these cases were civil. We can presume that the jury's right (or usurpation of right) was given even greater deference in criminal cases. The jurors of Massachusetts, however, could be reasonably fair. A case in point is that of eight British soldiers who were indicted as the sequel of the Boston Massacre. Five of the soldiers were acquitted by the jurors, and the remaining two, Kilroy and Montgomery, were found guilty of manslaughter only. The eighth defendant, Preston, was tried separately and was also acquitted.

The chief presiding judge was Trowbridge, who instructed the jurors to decide the law in issue as well as the evidence. Josiah Quincy, grandfather of the editor of the work cited in this chapter, was associated with John Adams in the defense. According to Quincy's reasoning, since the judge's summing up was for the defense, the jurors must take their law from the bench. Adams, consistent with his principles, still argued that the law was for the jurors, although in that course lay the real danger to his clients.[65] (This was four years before Adams was appointed chief justice of Massachusetts' revolutionary government, to succeed Trowbridge. He resigned, however, without taking his seat.[66]) Quincy says that even in civil matters, Massachusetts juries still had the right to decide law at the turn of the nineteenth century.[67]

Connecticut judges had been given the power to direct juries to find in accordance to the law, although a revision of

1702 did not contain this provision.[68] At the time of the revolution, the jurors of this state had the right to decide law and fact in both civil and criminal cases.[69] A case in 1788 held that the jury could not be mistaken in their verdict because the jurors were judges of both fact and law.[70] Their right in civil cases did not last long past 1800,[71] however.

Georgian jurors had the right to decide law by the constitutional enactment of 1777, but their constitution of 1789 did not retain the provision.[72] New Jersey had the right by a statute of 1676.[73] Juries had the right to decide law in New Hampshire[74] and early in Rhode Island[75], while in Vermont, the judges had very limited powers in both civil and criminal trials.[76] The right of the juries to decide law existed in Virginia, although it deteriorated in later years.[77] A judge in Maryland could send the jury back to deliberate if he thought the verdict wrong, or he could impanel another jury. If the second jury found contrary to the first, the judge could fine the first jury.[78] Maryland denied the privilege altogether in 1804,[79] but at least at the time of the Revolution in 1776, 10 of the 11 states for which we have found authority hold that the juries had the right to decide law.

The case of *Georgia* v. *Bailsford*, 3 U.S. 1 (1794), was tried to a special jury. The question was whether a debt due from Spalding belonged to the State of Georgia or to the original creditors. After hearing arguments for four days, Chief Justice Jay, in the first jury trial in the United States Supreme Court, told the jury that the facts were agreed by the parties and the judges were agreed on the law. It sounded like a case, under modern procedure, for a directed verdict or a similar remedy. Chief Justice Jay, however, charged the jury:

> It may not be amiss, here, Gentlemen, to remind you of the good rule, that, on questions of fact, it is the province of the jury, on questions of law, it is the province of the court to decide. But it must be observed that by the same law which recognizes this reasonable distribution of jurisdiction, you have nevertheless a right to take upon yourselves to judge of both, and to determine the law as well as the fact in controversy. On this and on every other occasion,

however, we have no doubt, you will pay the respect, which is due to the opinion of the court: For, as on the one hand, it is presumed, that juries are the best judges of facts; it is, on the other hand, presumable, that the courts are the best judges of law. But still both objects are lawfully within your power of decision.

The jury returned with a verdict for the defendants in accordance with the charge, but the case is a clear demonstration of the right of juries, under authority of the United States Supreme Court, to decide questions of law. No Supreme Court judge was to deny the right of juries to decide law, the constitutionality of a statute excepted, before 1835. It is obvious that, at least in practice, in both the federal and state governments, the American people began by reserving to themselves as jurors the right to judge both law and facts.

Chapter VII Footnotes

1. *Sources of Our Liberties*, Perry and Cooper, editors (American Bar Foundation, 1959), p. 44.

2. *Id.* at p. 34.

3. "The English Common Law In The Early American Colonies," collected in *Select Essays in Anglo-American Legal History* (Cambridge, 1899), p. 378.

4. Perry and Cooper, *op. cit.* at note 1, at pp. 151-56.

5. Perry and Cooper, *op. cit.* at note 1, at p. 185.

6. "The English Common Law," *op. cit.* at note 2, at pp. 390, 393.

7. *Id.* at p. 398.

8. Perry and Cooper, *op. cit.* at note 1, at p. 217.

9. "The English Common Law...," *op. cit.* at note 2, at p. 386.

10. *The American Jury*, Harry Kalven, Jr., and Hans Zeisel (Little, Brown and Company, Boston, 1966), p. 22.

11. *The Federalist*, Number 83, Alexander Hamilton (National Home Library Foundation, 1937), p. 546.

12. "Trial by Jury and the Reform of Civil Procedure," Austin Wakeman, 31 Harv. L. Rev. 669, at 676 (1918).

13. "Juries as Judges of Criminal Law," Mark DeWolfe Howe, 52 Harv. L. Rev. 582, at 591 (1939).

14. Perry and Cooper, *op. cit.* at note 1, at pp. 187-88.

15. "The English Common Law...," *op. cit.* at note 2, at p. 385.

16. "The English Common Law...," *op. cit.* at note 2, at p. 386.

17. "The English Common Law...," *op. cit.* at note 2, at p. 403.

18. Duncan v. Louisiana, dissent by Justice Harlan, 391 U.S. 145, at 191 (1968).

19. Wakeman, *op. cit.* at note 12, at p. 681.

20. *Report of Cases Argued and Adjudged in the Superior Court of Judicature of the Province of Massachusetts Bay,* Josiah Quincy, Jr. (Little, Brown and Company, Boston, 1865), p. 559.

21. "The English Common Law...," *op. cit.* at note 2, at p. 378.

22. Quincy, *op. cit.* at note 20, at p. 559.

23. *The Federalist, op. cit.* at note 11, at pp. 546-47.

24. Quincy, *op. cit.* at note 20, at p. 560.

25. *Capital Traction* v. *Hof,* 174 U.S. 1, at p. 9 (1898).

26. "The English Common Law...," *op. cit.* at note 2, at p. 378.

27. For example, *Ashton* v. *Ashton,* 1 Dallas 4 (1760), and *Tother* v. *Christian,* 1 Dallas 6 (1763).

28. *Duncan* v. *Louisiana, op. cit.* at note 18, at pp. 191-92.

29. *Sources of Our Liberties, op. cit.* at note 1, at p. 288.

30. Perry and Cooper, *op. cit.* at note 1, at p. 270.

31. Perry and Cooper, *op. cit.* at note 1, at p. 266.

32. Perry and Cooper, *op. cit.* at note 1, at pp. 290, 292, 295.

33. Perry and Cooper, *op. cit.* at note 1, at p. 312.

34. *The Complete Jefferson,* Saul K. Padover, editor (Duell, Soan & Pearce, Inc., New York, 1943), pp. 120-21; *Jefferson,* Saul K. Padover (London, 1942), p. 157.

35. *Federal Code Annotated,* (Bobbs-Merrill Co., 1950), Constitution vol. p. 7.

36. *Id.* at p. 9.

37. *Federal Code Annotated, op. cit.* at note 35, at pp. 14, 17.

38. Perry and Cooper, *op. cit.* at note 1, at pp. 328, 330.

39. Perry and Cooper, *op. cit.* at note 1, at pp. 338-39.

40. Perry and Cooper, *op. cit.* at note 1, at pp. 346, 348.

41. Perry and Cooper, *op. cit.* at note 1, at pp. 355-56.

42. Perry and Cooper, *op. cit.* at note 1, at pp. 362, 366.

43. Wakeman, *op. cit.* at note 12, at p. 678.

44. Perry and Cooper, *op. cit.* at note 1, at pp. 374, 376.

45. Perry and Cooper, *op. cit.* at note 1, at pp. 382, 384-85.

46. *The Federalist, op. cit.* at note 11, at p. 555.

47. *Constitutions of the United States, National and State,* for Columbia University (Oceana Publications, New York) under listing for Rhode Island.

48. Wakeman, *op. cit.* at note 12, at pp. 672-73.

49. *Federal Code Annotated, op. cit.* at note 35, at p. 25.

50. *The Federalist, op. cit.* at note 11, at p. 538.

51. *The Federalist, op. cit.* at note 11, at pp. 542-43.

52. *The Federalist, op. cit.* at note 11, at p. 543.

53. *Ibid.*

54. Howe, *op. cit.* at note 13, at p. 594.

55. Quincy, *op. cit.* at note 20, at p. 568.

56. Quincy, *op. cit.* at note 20, at p. 569.

57. Howe, *op. cit.* at note 13, at p. 587.

58. Quincy, *op. cit.* at note 20, at p. 568.

59. *A Complete Collection of State Trials and Proceedings For High Treason,* T.B. Howell, editor (T.C. Hansard, London, 1816), XVII-692.

60. *Id.* at XVII-672-692.

61. Quincy, *op. cit.* at note 20, at p. 558.

62. Quincy, *op. cit.* at note 20, at pp. 560, 565-66.

63. Quincy, *op. cit.* at note 20, at pp. 553-557.

64. Quincy, *op. cit.* at note 20, at p. 558.

65. Quincy, *op. cit.* at note 20, at pp. 564-65.

66. Quincy, *op. cit.* at note 20, at p. 567.

67. *Ibid.*

68. Howe, *op. cit.* at note 13, at p. 601.

69. Quincy, *op. cit.* at note 20, at p. 568.

70. Howe, *op. cit.* at note 13, at p. 601.

71. Howe, *op. cit.* at note 13, at pp. 601-02.

72. Howe, *op. cit.* at note 13, at p. 598.

73. Quincy, *op. cit.* at note 20, at p. 568.

74. "The English Common Law...," *op. cit.* at note 3, at p. 387.

75. Quincy, *op. cit.* at note 20, at p. 568.

76. Howe, *op. cit.* at note 13, at p. 591.

77. Quincy, *op. cit.* at note 20, at p. 569.

78. "The English Common Law...," *op. cit.* at note 2, at p. 400.

79. Quincy, *op. cit.* at note 20, at p. 569.

VIII
The Gift Rejected

According to Brunner, prior to 1790 the English jury had been confined to England and its sister systems.[1] Repp, in 1832, noted that the various constitutions which had been established in the nineteenth century were dissimilar in most respects except that the jury "...was a vital point."[2] The first jury came to France after the revolution of July, 1789, and by September 16, 1791, the Constituent Assembly adopted trial by jury in criminal cases.[3] Robespierre urged the adoption of the civil jury, but it was rejected.[4] During the Reign of Terror, juries became permanent commissions, although even this formality of a trial was soon dropped.[5]

When the "terror" had ended, the jury was re-established.[6] Napoleon retained the criminal jury in his Code of 1808, but there was no grand jury in France except for the period from 1791 to 1808. Criminal proceedings were commenced by the prosecutor who presented crimes to the Judge d'Instruction (generally three judges who could bring charges on their own initiative).[7] At this time, a unanimous verdict was required except when the jury had deliberated for more than 24 hours.[8] Jurors were required to be at least 30, and service was limited to those with the electoral franchise, and those from selected categories including retired military officers, physicians, lawyers and notaries.[9] It was said that Napoleon required his officers to select jurors for service that were predisposed in his favor.[10]

After the Revolution of 1848, participation in jury service was extended. It was still required, however, that jurors be 30 years of age and able to read and write. Bankrupts, felons and state employees were excluded, and persons over 70 and those dependent on their daily labor could be excused on request.[11] Beginning in 1832, the jury was permitted to accompany a verdict of "guilty" with an additional claim of extenuating circumstances.[12] The difficulty with this type of verdict is that the quantum of proof necessary for conviction is reduced by inducing juries to compromise. The jury survived Louis Napoleon, with alteration; e.g., judges were instructed in 1880 to dispense with summing up,[13] and unanimity had been dispensed with, first for two-thirds and then, in 1853, for a simple majority.

The French jury was reduced in number in 1932, and, after the verdict, the jurors were permitted to consult with the judge on the penalty if there had been a conviction. As a result of this last provision, the percentage of convictions rose.[14] The Vichy government enacted in 1943 that the jury would thereafter deliberate on guilt or innocence with the judge. From this time, although called jurors, the lay members of the court were really assessors. This system was retained after the war. Today, the French jurors or lay assessors sit with three professional judges, and the decision is made by a simple majority. The jurors are still required to be over 30 and able to read and write.[15]

As can be seen from the material in the first three chapters, in early times Germany had institutions in which the lay element was present in the judging process in various degrees. For example, there were vestiges of northern juries in Germany in the late Middle Ages. Also, Hauenstein's charter of 1442 secured the right of being tried by a jury of 24 jurors in both civil and criminal cases.[16] A Swabian ordinance of 1562 provided for trials by a jury of 12, whereas Emmendinger had trials by a tribunal of 12 headmen. As late as 1748, a criminal jury trial was held at Purlach in the Grand Duchy of Baden.[17] Gradually, however, trial by judge alone became the rule. The judge relied on secret investigations, written records and interrogation of the accused, alone and without counsel. The process lasted as long as one and one-half years and the accused often spent that time in jail.[18] A comparison with Kafka's *Trial* indicates that this novel about judicial terror was based on fact.

The German jury of the nineteenth century was not descended from these earlier German models. Instead, the modern jury came to the German Rhineland when it was invaded by the French in 1798, and after the French left, the Rhenish people continued the tradition. Prussia, however, was opposed to the jury because of its French origin. A commission composed of two Rhenish and three Prussian members investigated the jury in 1819 and unanimously recommended that it be retained. This was done although political offenses were exempted from its jurisdiction.[19]

As a consequence of the political disturbances of 1848, trial by jury was adopted in various German states, such as Bavaria Hesse in 1848, Wurtemburg in 1849 and Austria in 1850. These juries were similar to the French model; i.e., the jurors had to be taxpayers of a certain level or members of certain professions and at least 30 years old. There was no grand jury. A verdict agreed by seven out of 12 was sufficient. If the court thought a verdict of guilty erroneous, it could order a new trial, although only once.[20]

Germany dispensed with the jury in 1924. Serious crimes were then tried by a court consisting of six members and three judges.[21] They made one bench, voting jointly with majority rule. Jurors, or assessors, on this court sat one time only. For less serious charges, one judge sat with two lay assessors who served for two-year terms. These last assessors were appointed only with a view to their qualifications. These tribunals continued to dispense justice in Germany until the present day, with the exception of World War II, during which all courts were finally abolished.[22]

Elsewhere in Europe, Belgium introduced jury trial in 1830, at which time the chances of acquittal immediately doubled. Holland had the jury for awhile after 1831,[23] while Portugal introduced the jury to some degree in 1832 and more fully in 1837. The number of jurors was limited to six in 1840, and a vote of two-thirds was sufficient for a verdict. In addition, the judges could review the verdicts and order new trials if they were not satisfied.[24] Greece first used the jury trial in 1834 and retained it in the constitution of 1843. Geneva obtained jury trial in 1844 and Sardinia in 1850,[25] ten years before Italy,[26] where it was abolished in 1931.[27] Russia established jury trial in 1864[28] and abandoned it under Communist rule as did her satellites and Yugoslavia.[29]

Denmark seems to have a type of jury where the judge could insist on acquittal if he disagreed with a verdict of guilty.[30]

Sweden makes use of lay judges in the way the English use justices of the peace, and the jury was only used when the case involved freedom of the press.[31] Japan adopted the jury along with other western innovations, but suspended it in 1943 and never revived it after the war.[32]

We would expect to find the jury introduced into most places where British influence was strong. For example, an attempt was made to introduce the jury to India in 1832.[33] Canada, naturally, uses the jury, but in modern times, except in Ontario, the civil jury has ceased to exist for the most part.[34] In Australia, a jury is used in personal injury cases except in South Australia and New South Wales. A majority verdict was used in Tasmania and New South Wales before it was introduced into England in the late 1960's.[35] In South Australia, a majority of 10 out of 12 is sufficient for conviction or acquittal after four hours of deliberation, and in Tasmania after two hours of deliberation.[36]

The jury adopted by Malta in 1854 consisted of nine jurors who could reach a verdict when six were agreed, and the judge was permitted to order a new trial if he thought the verdict erroneous.[37] The discretion lies with the government in Nyasaland to decide whether an offense requires a jury.[38] The membership of a Kenyan jury is restricted to the Europeans in those cases in which the accused is European, while, on the other hand, South Africa prohibits non-Europeans from serving on juries. When non-whites are defendants or accusers, the Minister of Justice has authority to order the case tried to a judge and two assessors, although the usual South African criminal jury consists of nine members, seven of whom must concur for a verdict.[39]

As far as the British Isles were concerned, the Scots had used the jury almost as early as England, but the civil jury was gradually lost through lack of use. A case involving the right to land was tried by 12 persons who were sworn and gave a verdict in 1469, although in 1532, the Scotland Court of Session, consisting of 15 members, was instituted, and it was thought to have a large enough membership so that a jury would not be needed. The Sheriff's Court at Orkney, however, tried both civil and criminal cases by jury during the years 1602 to 1604. Although the early Scots retained the criminal jury, they only required a bare majority for a verdict.[40]

Civil juries were reintroduced into Scotland in 1807, and a general statute was enacted in 1815 as an experiment which proved successful, and trial by jury was therefore made permanent after seven years. The civil jury consisted of 12 members whose verdict was required to be unanimous, contrasting with the criminal jury which had 15 members and could render a verdict by a bare majority. If the civil jury deliberated for more than 12 hours, they were discharged unless they requested more time. In 1852, the length of required deliberation was reduced to six hours. In fact, one of the main reasons for reintroducing civil juries into Scotland was to discourage appeals.[41]

Although the civil jury has not proven popular in Scotland, personal injury cases there are still tried by a jury, although not in England. In criminal cases, the jurors have the choice of three verdicts: guilty, not guilty and not proven.[42] The jury is also used in Scotland in almost the same form as the original Frankish and Norman inquisitions. For example, after six teenagers died on the slopes of the Cairngorm Mountains in central Scotland in late November, 1971, the investigation of the tragedy was conducted by a sheriff before a jury of seven.[43]

Not unexpectedly, the jury thrived in a special way in Ireland. That country had the highest rate of acquittals (45.3%) of the criminal juries rendering verdicts during 1850. This was more than double the acquittal rate for England and almost double the acquittal rate for Scotland for the same year.[44] There can be little doubt that this high percentage of acquittals can be attributed largely to the political disaffection of the Irish.

It had seemed by the 1850's that the jury was going to become a hallmark of western civilization. In fact, in the 1970's, we find that even the criminal jury is very much restricted to countries that are still or have been dominated by England. The only non-Anglo-Saxon countries using the criminal jury in 1966 were Austria, Belgium, Denmark, Greece, Norway and some parts of Switzerland and Latin America, with the limited use noted for Sweden.[45] Even at the height of the jury's popularity, no continental country introduced the jury as a mode of trial for civil cases.[46] The lay assessor system, which we have seen is popular in criminal cases on the continent, is quite a different thing than the English jury. What remains now is to trace the development of the jury in England and the United States during the nineteenth and twentieth centuries.

Chapter VIII Footnotes

1. *The Origin of Juries*, Heinrich Brunner (Berlin, 1872), p. 78.

2. *Trial by Jury, Wager of Law and Co-ordinate Forensic Institutions*, Thorl. Gudn. Repp (Thomas Clarke, Edinburgh, 1832), p. 59.

3. *History of Trial By Jury*, William Forsyth (John W. Parker and Son, London, 1852), p. 347.

4. *Id.* at p. 364.

5. Forsyth, *op. cit.* at note 3, at p. 347.

6. *Ibid.*

7. Forsyth, *op. cit.* at note 3, at p. 348.

8. Forsyth, *op. cit.* at note 3, at p. 347.

9. Forsyth, *op. cit.* at note 3, at p. 352.

10. *Democracy In America*, Alexis Clerel DeTocqueville, translated by Henry Reeve (New York, 1838), p. 283.

11. Forsyth, *op. cit.* at note 3, at p. 354.

12. "The Jury Abroad," anonymous, 221 The Law Times 118(1956).

13. *Ibid.*

14. *Ibid.*

15. *Ibid.*

16. Forsyth, *op. cit.* at note 3, at p. 370.

17. Forsyth, *op. cit.* at note 3, at p. 370.

18. Forsyth, *op. cit.* at note 3, at pp. 371, 373-75.

19. Forsyth, *op. cit.* at note 3, at pp. 382-83.

20. Forsyth, *op. cit.* at note 3, at pp. 384-85.

21. *The Jury*, W.R. Cornish (The Penguin Press, London, 1968), p. 269.

22. "The Jury Abroad," *op. cit.* at note 12, at p. 118.

23. Forsyth, *op. cit.* at note 3, at pp. 365, 460.

24. Forsyth, *op. cit.* at note 3, at p. 366.

25. Forsyth, *op. cit.* at note 3, at pp. 366-67.

26. "The Jury Abroad," *op. cit.* at note 12, at p. 118.

27. Cornish, *op. cit.* at note 21, at p. 135.

28. *The American Jury*, Harry Kalven, Jr. and Hans Zeisel (Little, Brown and Company, Boston, 1966), p. 4.

29. *The Proof of Guilt*, Glanville Williams (Stevens and Sons, 1963 ed, 1st Ed. 1955), p. 255.

30. Williams, *Id.* at p. 334.

31. Williams, *op. cit.* at note 29, at pp. 256, 298.

32. Williams, *op. cit.* at note 29, at pp. 254-55.

33. Forsyth, *op. cit.* at note 3, at p. 448.

34. "Preservation of the Civil Jury," Stanley E. Stacks, 22 Wash. & Lee L. Rev. 76, at 80-81.

35. "Address by The Right Honourable Lord Denning," 11 Australian L.J. 224, at 226 (1967).

36. Williams, *op. cit.* at note 29, at p. 320.

37. *Ibid.*

38. Williams, *op. cit.* at note 29, at p. 262.

39. Williams, *op. cit.* at note 29, at pp. 262-63, 320.

40. Forsyth, *op. cit.* at note 3, at pp. 303-06, 332.

41. Forsyth, *op. cit.* at note 3, at pp. 303, 308-11, 323, 325.

42. Cornish, *op. cit.* at note 21, at pp. 259, 292.

43. *Manchester Guardian*, February 9, 1972, p. 6.

44. Forsyth, *op. cit.* at note 3, at pp. 458-9.

45. Kalven and Zeisel, *op. cit.* at note 28, at p. 13.

46. Forsyth, *op. cit.* at note 3, at p. 434.

IX
Inconvenient Relic
(England — 1789-1973)

At the time of the French Revolution, the starting point for the worldwide spread of the jury, the English still had other ancient modes of trial. Although seldom used, such practices as wager of law (compurgation), trial by battle, the possessory assizes and other ancient trappings had never been officially repealed. During the remaining two centuries of the jury's story, almost all ancient procedures were eliminated.

Judicial combat was abolished in 1819.[1] The last trial by wager of law was held in 1824, and this form of trial was eliminated by statute in 1833.[2] Attaint, seldom used for more than a century, was revoked in 1825, and thus would no longer be a threat to jurors.[3] Fifty-six courts of the hundreds still existed in the 1830's, but they were little used. The Leet Court of Manchester became the government of the city of Manchester, although it was still the property of a private lord. The town council bought the court from the lord who owned it for the hefty price of 200,000 pounds, and it was allowed to disappear.[4]

The possessory assizes (novel disseisin, mort d'ancestor, darrein presentment) were eliminated in 1833, but, because of a pending action, the last meeting of the Grand Assize was held in 1838. Four knights, together with swords, and 12 other recognitors acted as the jury in common pleas court.[5] The unique jury for foreign parties, the jury *per medietate linguae*, was permitted to pass out of existence.[6] Special juries, both praised and criticised, were to remain for a longer time. In order to become a special juror, it was necessary to be a person legally entitled to be called esquire, or a person of high degree, such as a banker, a merchant, the head of a dwelling rated at not less than 100 pounds in a town of 20,000 or 50 pounds elsewhere, and so on.[7] Special jurors were more likely to vote with the crown than the ordinary juror in the hope of being chosen again in order to earn more money — thus the name "guinea men."[8] Special juries were abolished, however, in 1949 with limited exceptions.[9] No trial with a special jury has been held since 1954.[10]

The remaining ancient mode of trial, trial by jury, seemed to have a more promising future. Fox's libel bill, passed in 1792, gave English juries an absolute right to deliver a general verdict in libel prosecutions. It is not clear that this changed the law at all, aside from preventing the forcing of a special verdict upon the jury by an overbearing judge. In part, it reads:

> the jury ... may give a general verdict of guilty or not guilty upon the whole matter put in issue [providing the court or judge] shall, according to their or his discretion give their directions to the jury on the matter in issue ... in like matter as in other criminal cases.[11]

Confidence in the jury was on the rise, and in 1837 the jury was chosen to set values in cases of eminent domain.[12] As contrasted with American practice, divorce cases were tried by jury at this time. For example, juries in England tried divorce cases when requested by parties pursuant to legislation passed in 1857. Probate matters were also tried to juries on request by 1857, and the chancery court could order a jury if requested by a party as early as 1858. In fact, by 1900, 50 percent of the divorce cases were tried by jury. However, although a jury trial in a divorce case is still a possibility, the last time this occurred was in 1956.[13]

The jury's jurisdiction was expanded in 1888 when minor civil suits in county courts could be tried to juries upon demand.[14] The next century, however, found the jury struggling to hold its ground rather than develop new areas. After the abolition of juries in civil cases in 1918, jury trial was restored with certain exceptions in 1925. This restoration was to last only until 1933 when a general right to a civil jury was again abolished, except in matters involving fraud.[15]

There were more losses than gains as far as jury trial was concerned. A seemingly insignificant statute was passed in 1854 giving parties the right to waive juries in common pleas court.[16]

(Previously, the only trials in this court were jury trials.) This statute was enacted in the hope that other ends could be achieved by limiting jury trials. But even such statutes as this one put some pressure on counsel to choose court trial, not as the most desirable mode of trial, but in order not to offend the judiciary.

On the criminal side of the docket, summary trial before a magistrate was permitted by an 1855 statute if the defendant waived the jury charges of stealing where the value involved was less than five shillings. The amount was raised to two pounds in 1879, 20 pounds in 1915 and removed entirely in 1962 when summary trial of other crimes was also permitted.[17] Devlin claimed in the 1966 edition of *Trial by Jury* that 85 per cent of the indictable offenses were tried summarily by magistrates without a jury at the defendant's request.[18] (Occasionally, the consent of the prosecution was also obtained, although it was not mandatory).[19]

According to Cornish, in 1965, 88 percent of offenders were handled in magistrate court without a jury.[20] These figures most certainly include guilty pleas, but, even so, they appear to indicate that the jury is not popular with criminal defendants. This is misleading, however, as the defendants are offered an enticement to choose summary trial. The sentencing power of magistrates court is generally limited to a maximum of six months and a 400 pound fine. A case could be referred to Quarter Sessions for a stiffer sentence, but this does not seem to be the rule.[21] Quite apart from any jurisdictional sentencing differential, it is common practice in the United States for defendants to waive a jury trial in order to be given a break in sentencing. This is well known to the lawyers and is one of the chief considerations in inducing pleas of guilty. Logically, however, there can be no equitable reason for requiring a stiffer penalty in the one case than in the other.

In 1873, the common pleas courts were given power to refer to referees matters requiring prolonged examination, such as the investigation of documents, accounts, or scientific and other investigation.[22] In point of theory, this could have diminished the jurisdiction of the jury, but it does not appear that this power was widely used. After 1883, jury trial was used in ordinary course only in cases of libel, slander, malicious prosecution, seduction, false imprisonment and breach of promise. In other cases, a party desiring jury trial had to request it, the aim being to reduce the number of jury trials necessary. As a result of this act, in the areas where a request was necessary, jury trials fell from 80 percent to 50 percent of the total.[23]

As a war measure, jury trial in civil cases was abolished except in the six cases mentioned in the 1883 act.[24] Jury trial was restored in 1925, but this lasted only until 1933 when this statute became law:

Sec. 1 ... grand juries are hereby abolished....

Sec. 6. (1) Subject as hereinafter provided, if on the application of any party to be tried in the King's Bench Division of the High Court made not later than such time before the trial as may be limited by rules of court, the court or a judge is satisfied that—

(a) A charge of fraud against that party; or

(b) A claim in respect libel, slander, malicious prosecution, false imprisonment, seduction or breach of promise of marriage is in issue, the action shall be order to be tried with a jury unless the court of judge is of the opinion that the trial thereof requires prolonged examination of documents or accounts or any scientific or local investigation which cannot conveniently be made with a jury; but save as aforesaid, any action to be tried in that division may, in the discretion of the court or a judge, be ordered to be tried either with or without a jury:

Provided that the provisions of this section shall be without prejudice to the power of the court or a judge to order in accordance with rules of court, that different questions of fact arising in any actions be tried by different modes of trial, and where any such order is made the provisions of this section requiring trial with a jury in certain cases shall have effect only as respects questions relating to any such charge or claim as aforesaid.[25]

Nothing in this statute seems to require the virtual elimination of jury trials, but that was to be its effect.

From about 1939, the great majority of accident-injury cases was tried by judge alone,[26] and in fact, from 1954 to 1964, less than 20 such cases were tried by juries in England.[27] In these cases, the jury awards ran generally higher than similar awards by judges,[28] and Cornish estimated that in approximately one-third of the cases the jury awards were markedly higher than those by a judge alone, while in about one-third of the cases, jury awards were lower.[29] Verdicts for quadreplegic cases in 1962-63 were about 50,000 punds ($120,000), it being estimated that judges would have rendered awards for such cases ranging from 30 to 35,000 pounds.[30] In one case in 1972, a 17-year-old girl was awarded 59,000 pounds for permanent brain injuries which would prevent her from performing all but the simplest household tasks.[31] This trial was held without a jury, like all such cases since 1964.

Among the reasons considered as rendering juries unfit to try personal injury cases were: (1) the cases were overly complicated; (2) the time and expense were greater with a jury; (3) it was impossible to achieve uniformity with juries; (4) it was difficult to control jury verdict on appeal; and (5) it is improper for the jury to consider the fact that the defendant is insured as this fact often prejudices the jurors.[32] Referring to that part of the 1933 statute which provided that trial could be had by jury at the discretion of the trial judge, Judge Salmon, concurring in the Watts decision, said:

> I must confess that, if I were approaching the matter res integra, I should have thought that the section, and the rules passed in pursuance of it, confer an unfettered discretion on the judge to order or refuse a jury as he thought fit. In 1937, this court, ... decided ... that that was exactly what the section did mean.

Judge Salmon would have overruled *Sims* v. *William Howard* (the first case holding that juries were not proper tribunals for personal injury cases),[33] but he joined in the instant decision which merely affirmed the decision of the trial court to sit with-

out a jury.[34] The *Sims* and *Watts* decisions put an end to trials of
personal injury cases by juries in England. The atrophy of trial
by jury was not limited to personal injury. Even in 1963, only
one and one-half percent of the cases tried by the Queen's
Bench were tried by a jury. (This court does not ordinarily try
criminal cases.)[35] This percentage was approximately the same
in 1965 and 1966.[36]

For those jurors who were still required, statutes had been
passed which ameliorated their condition. At the discretion of
the judge, after 1870 jurors were permitted to use a fire when
out of the courtroom and to have reasonable refreshments at
their own expense.[37] After 1897, the jury was permitted to separate at night except in murder cases, although after 1940 they
were allowed to do so except during the summing up and deliberation period.[38] In 1949, jurors were finally paid travel and sub-
sistence expenses, plus an allowance for loss of earnings, not to
exceed 20 shillings a day.[39] The limit on the amount allowed for
loss of earnings was removed in 1954,[40] and by 1968, the jurors
could get up to six pounds and 10 shillings a day for loss of earnings.[41]

A number of statutes relating to the jury were purely administrative in character. A statute of 1825 specified qualifications for jurors, such as an age requirement between 21 and
60, a property requirement, and the provision that the juror
must be a resident of that county. A view could be held with the
stipulation that, although a majority of jurors must be present
at the view, the entire number was not necessary. In addition,
jurors would receive a certificate of service in return for payment of a shilling to the sheriff.[42] Many courts in the United
States give similar certificates to jurors at the conclusion of
their term. Also, the practice of the king asking jurors to stand
aside in lieu of challenging was reaffirmed,[43] although peremptory common law challenges in murder, treason, and piracy
cases were limited to 20.[44] The Criminal Justice Act of 1947 provided that the defendant could only have seven peremptory
challenges.[45] A defendant remaining silent when charged with
treason, a felon or a misdemeanor was treated as though he had
pleaded guilty and the trial proceeded.[46] With the consent of the

parties, a verdict could be rendered by less than 12 jurors after 1851.[47]

Women, except in connection with determining pregnancy, were not permitted to serve on juries until 1919. That act provided:

> 1. ...and a person shall not be exempted by sex or marriage from liability to serve as a juror: Provided that ... (b) Any judge, chairman of quarter sessions, recorder or other person before whom a case is or may be heard may, in his discretion, on application made by or on behalf of the parties (including in criminal cases the prosecution and the accused or any of them, or at his own instance), make an order that the jury shall be composed of men only or women only as the case may require, or may, on an application made by a woman to be exempted from service on a jury in respect of any case by reason of the nature of the evidence to be given or of the issues to be tried, grant, such exemption.[48]

The statute also provided for exemption for those women jurors unfit for service for medical reasons. Therefore, juries continued to consist primarily of men, women amounting to only about 11 percent of those serving in the 1960's.[49] Women also lost their right to exclusively determine whether women convicted of capital crimes were pregnant. This question would be decided instead by the jury trying the principal offense; if this was impossible, another jury would be chosen for this purpose.[50] By a statute of 1965, at the discretion of the court, trial of a case could continue despite the illness or unavoidable inability of a juror to continue as long as nine jurors remained. This act amended a 1925 act which had required 10 jurors to be present and also required the consent of the defendant and the crown.[51]

Some changes in trial procedures had to do with the type of evidence the judge or jury could consider. One change was the increasing use of expert witnesses. A handwriting expert was permitted to testify in a criminal case in 1865 and in a civil case in 1854.[52] By a statute of 1907, the court of criminal appeals was given the power to appoint experts, although it never exercised the power.[53] In 1916, a chemist was permitted to testify in his expert capacity in a will contest case,[54] while in another case the results of an electroencephalography test were permitted as expert testimony concerning epilepsy in 1940.[55]

Some changes seemed to have helped the crown more than the defense. Most defense counsel agree that the power of the judge to sum up facts and law, while giving his own opinion without binding the jury, is a procedure favorable to conviction. This power was granted by statute in 1841, although previously, in the eighteenth century, the practice had arisen of the judge only summing up the law.[56]

A change of the utmost significance was contained in the Criminal Justice Act of 1967. It provided for the possibility of a majority verdict; e.g., if there were 11 or 12 jurors, 10 could return a verdict, or, if there were only 10 jurors, nine could return a verdict. It was necessary for the jurors to have deliberated for at least two hours, at which time the judge at his discretion was permitted to authorize the jury to return a majority verdict.[57] This type of verdict helps the crown in two ways. It almost entirely eliminates the protection the unanimity rule gives to minority populations. Even a minority as large as 20 percent of the population has only a small chance of being on the jury panel because of property qualifications in England and because of the crown's right to have jurors stand aside. Assuming that a member of the defendant's minority group was impanelled, the majority verdict nonetheless meant that he would have little influence on the jury's final decision.

The other way that a majority verdict is favorable to the crown is that it makes it more likely that a verdict will be reached. Two hung juries are tantamount to acquittal, not to conviction, and often, a case was not retried after one hung jury. Since it is the crown that is the moving party, the defense accomplishes most of its objectives with a hung jury. The majority verdict decreases the quantum of proof necessary for a conviction by reason of these considerations. This same act (Act of 1967), also provided that the defendant had to give advanced notice of his intention to use an alibi.[58]

Some changes in procedure were in the defendant's favor. It was enacted in 1836 that the defendant could be fully represented by counsel at all stages of criminal proceedings, including argument to the jury.[59] After 1848, justices were required to warn the criminal defendant that he need not give evidence against himself,[60] although the defendant himself was finally permitted to testify under oath after 1898. From the dates of these last two statutes, it would appear that the crown had somehow been permitted to question the defendant even before the 1898 act. Prior to 1898, however, some justices had allowed defendants to make an unsworn statement. After the act of 1898 was passed, the defendant was not required to testify, but, if he did, he could be cross-examined by counsel for the crown. The defendant can still make an unsworn statement from the box, but this is not often done because such a statement lacks credibility.[61] Also, by the nineteenth century, the indigent defendant was provided counsel at the expense of the government.[62]

Anyone attending a criminal trial at the Old Bailey at the present time would immediately notice that the barristers and the judge wear robes and wigs. The courtroom is arranged so that solicitors are permitted to sit at tables on two sides between the barristers and the jury, while the defendant and judge are seated on the other two sides. If the case is of some importance, there are generally two barristers for the crown and two for each defendant. The jurors are nearly all men, the greater number of them being past their forties. The jurors, contrary to most jurisdictions in the United States, are permitted to take notes and are provided with paper for this purpose. It is interesting to observe, however, that the jurors seldom make use of this privilege. Only one counsel stands at a time, and aside from going to the dock to talk with his client (who remains more or less caged during the entire trial), he seldom leaves his seat. If counsel desires a witness to examine a document, it is conveyed to the witness by an official of the court. The witness is required to remain standing during the delivery of his testimony.

English counsel tend to phrase their terminology differently than their American counterparts; for example, in contradicting a witness, an English barrister will say, "I put it to you that what really happened was...." English lawyers make few objections to the proceedings, although the bench intervenes frequently for the sake of clarity, rather than for any need to keep order.

The senior counsel is called a Queen's Counsel, and he is required to associate himself with a junior. Generally, a barrister can apply to become Queen's Counsel after being in practice for about 10 years. This is not necessarily an attractive proposition, however, since it necessitates an increase in his fees, in addition to having to associate with a junior. The barristers do not belong to law firms as such, but they may share chambers and the services of a clerk with an assistant. Barristers receive their cases through the work of solicitors, who are not permitted to practice in the High Court or at Old Bailey, although they can form partnerships and practice in the lower courts.

A difference in the approach to trial may also be noted from the time jurors are called to be sworn. If they are to be challenged, it must be before they are sworn. As opposed to American practice, challenges are infrequently used because barristers and clients lack information on which to challenge intelligently, and because the custom has developed to not challenge except in exceptional cases. In 1964, out of 110 total cases, 25 jurors were challenged in 14 cases.[63] A similar report mentioned by Devlin alleged that challenges were used in 24 out of 341 cases (50 jurors challenged out of 4,092).[64] In an exceptional case at Old Bailey in October and November of 1971, there were multiple black defendants and all of their challenges (seven each) were used in order to obtain black jurors. Generally, however, the observation by an experienced barrister to the effect that, "In England, the trial begins when the jury is picked; in the United States, the trial is over when the jury is picked," has a great deal of truth.

The burden of proof in a civil case involves the "balance of probabilities,"[65] while in criminal cases, the burden of proof is "beyond a reasonable doubt."[66] This was not clear in the late forties and early fifties, however, when it was thought that the burden of proof was that the jury must be "satisfied of guilt," and so on.[67] The crown cannot cross-examine the defendant about his past record unless he has attacked the credibility of crown witnesses.[68] A wife cannot be compelled to testify against her husband, and in fact cannot testify against him at all except for the usual matters including offenses against her or her children.[69]

It is unusual for English juries to deliberate more than four to five hours, and the percentage of disagreements was small even before the introduction of majority verdicts.[70] The overall impression gained from observing both civil and criminal trials in London is the apparent detachment on the part of counsel, the judge, the jury, and even the parties. This atmosphere is looked upon as a great virtue by the English bar, but one can't help feeling, however, that this lack of interest in the proceedings would be a disadvantage to the client as far as the jury was concerned. This air of detachment begins even before the trial commences because the solicitor does most of the trial preparation, such as interviewing witnesses, which the barrister is generally forbidden to do (except for the client and expert witnesses). Even the solicitor, especially in criminal cases, must be very circumspect about interviewing witnesses. He most certainly would not interview persons known to be crown witnesses without notifying the police and counsel for the other side, as well as having a third party present. (This holds true despite the fact that the Law Society (the ruling association to which solicitors belong) has ruled that witnesses are not the property of either the Crown or the defendant, and both parties should have equal access to them.) Very rarely would a witness for the crown be interviewed out of court by the defense after the witness had testified at a preliminary hearing.[71]

In the capacity of a consultant, the writer was asked to sit in at a pre-trial conference in a barrister's office which was being held preparatory to trial. All who were present were the barrister, a junior, two solicitors and the client, in addition to the writer, while a witness who showed up was asked to leave by the barrister. The barrister had already read the solicitor's brief, but did not have a firm grasp of the details of the case, although trial was to commence the following Monday. The barrister was shown for the first time several dozen police photographs which the solicitor had recently obtained, but nothing was done about having several photographs which were favorable to the defendant blown up for use as exhibits. The defendant was not questioned at all, but there was simply an exchange of views and information between the barrister, the solicitors and the client. The entire conference lasted about an hour and a half, and this constituted most of the trial preparation at which the client was present. In spite of what would have been inadequate preparation under American procedures, the client was acquitted.

As to the impact jury service makes on the citizens, in 1964 approximately seven million citizens in England and Wales were eligible for service.[72] About 175,000 were actually called for service and 110,000 impanelled for duty,[73] while approximately 5,000 to 6,000 cases are tried a year.[74] By far the greater number of the cases tried are criminal cases, as the civil jury in England is practically extinct. It is likely that soon the property qualification will be dropped and eligibility for jury service will begin at the age of 18 with the passage of the Criminal Justice Act of 1972.[75] Although there would therefore be more jurors, they would have less to do. Libel is one of the remaining strongholds of the civil jury, but the Law Society has recommended that the jury no longer be permitted to fix damages in libel cases.[76] In England, there is no new trial in criminal matters if there is a conviction. (The right to order a new trial may have been recently enacted, but if so, it has not been acted upon).[77] A judge, in contrast to a juror, has no maximum age unless he is newly appointed, in which case his maximum age is 75.

The coroner's jury has remained in very much the same form for many years, although the number of jurors serving on a particular coroner's jury has varied. Before 1926, it was between 12 and 23. Since then, there are 7 to 11 members, and they can deliver a verdict if no more than two dissent from the verdict. Coroner's juries are responsible for returning verdicts in unexplained death such as murder, manslaughter and infanticide. If indicated by a verdict, the coroner must issue arrest warrants. If criminal proceedings are instituted previous to a verdict, however, the coroner's proceeding is adjourned.[78]

We find an even purer form of the ancient jury existing in London at the present time. This is the Trial of the Pyx. The "Pyx" is a box in which samples of coins minted by the Royal Mint are placed. Once a year, a jury of goldsmiths is called upon to try the quality of the coin of the realm. The first record of such a trial in England was in 1248, but it became almost the exclusive responsibility of the goldsmiths from 1349. From the time of Elizabeth I, the trial took the form that it still retains.[79] On March 10, 1972, this writer attended the Trial of the Pyx at the Goldsmith's Hall. On arriving, the armoured truck was already present and 30 some boxes containing coins and trial plates were being unloaded. The jurors soon began to assemble, including men in high positions such as heads of financial institutions, experts from the assay office and some retired persons, but all free men of the Goldsmith's Company.

The 26 jurors seated themselves around a long table in a decorative, baroque room. The Queen's Remembrancer, an officer of the Exchequer and a high judicial officer, arrived precisely on time in wig and robe, accompanied by his aides. He administered an oath to the jurors who had been supplied testaments for this purpose. The jurors elected a foreman, and the Queen's Remembrancer addressed the jurors regarding their duty. After this was done, the jury was adjourned until April 21, 1972, when their verdict would be delivered. Immediately upon adjournment, the members set at once to their task, opening packets of 10 and 50 pence pieces, counting them, and putting two of those coins from each packet into a wooden bowl to be later subjected to exacting tests. Part of the jury had departed to another room to count the five pence pieces with automatic machines, an innovation of the preceding year. Of the five pence pieces, only one from each packet was saved for further testing.

Other jurors were in another part of the Goldsmith's Hall operating huge and sensitive balances. They weighed all the coins and the trial plates. When they had completed these tasks, they had refreshments provided by the Goldsmith's Company. They would also be treated to a dinner after they returned their final verdict.

This then was the state to which the English jury had declined since the peak of its power in the last half of the nineteenth century. In 1971, it appeared that even libel cases would often be ordered tried without the benefit of a jury. On March 19, 1971, *The Times* carried an article under the headline, "Profit and Dishonour in Fleet Street." The article charged certain interests with heartlessly closing down a great newspaper for profit and needlessly bringing unemployment to hundreds. *The Times*, its editor and the reporter were sued for libel by Associated Newspapers Group and others, and the case is reported as *Rothermere et al v. Times Newspapers Ltd. et al.*[80]

The Times requested jury trial and, initially, the request was granted. An interlocutory appeal was allowed, however, and trial was directed to be by a judge sitting alone, on the ground that "...the trial would require a prolonged examination of documents and accounts which could not be conveniently made with a jury." *The Times* appealed from this order to the Court of Appeal.[81]

By a majority of two to one, the Court of Appeal held that *The Times* was entitled to a jury trial. Lord Denning and Lord Lawton wrote the majority opinions. Lord Lawton said,

> If the defendants lost their action and heavy damages were awarded against them, the newspaper scene in this country might never be the same again. The reputation which *The Times* had enjoyed for so long around the world for responsible journalism would be badly dented, if not destroyed. The destruction of its reputation would be the destruction of a national institution. A trial which could have that result should not be the responsibility of one man.[82]

This decision was of immense importance to the limited retention of the civil jury in England. Leave to appeal to the House of Lords was denied.[83] England's great libel trials will continue to be tried to 12 jurors. Perhaps Englishmen really do believe that the jury is the best tribunal for determining facts, but they only resort to trial by judge alone as a matter of convenience while reserving the jury for matters touching their honor.

Chapter IX Footnotes

1. *The History of English Law*, Sir Fredrick Pollock and Frederick William Maitland (2nd edition, Cambridge Univ. Press, 1895), I-150.

2. *A Preliminary Treatise on Evidence*, James Bradley Thayer (Sweet and Maxwell, London, 1898), pp. 33-34.

3. *Id.* at p. 152.

4. *A History of Lay Judges*, John P. Dawson (Harvard Univ. Press, Cambridge, Mass., 1960), pp. 183, 253-54.

5. *History of Trial By Jury*, William Forsyth (John W. Parker and Son, London, 1852), p. 139.

6. *Id.* at p. 345, seemingly in conflict with the statement at p. 230, but this form of the jury was gone.

7. *The Statutes Revised*, 1870, 33 and 34 Vict. C77.

8. *The Jury*, W.R. Cornish (The Penguin Press, London, 1968), p. 131.

9. *The Statutes Revised*, Juries Act, 1949, Sec. 18(1) a.

10. Cornish, *op. cit.* at note 8, at p. 32-33.

11. "Juries as Judges of Criminal Law," Mark De Wolfe Howe, 52 Harv. L. Rev. 582, at 585 (1939).

12. *The Statutes Revised*, 1837 C. 94 sec. 19.

13. Cornish, *op. cit.* at note 8, at p. 75.

14. *Ibid.*

15. *Trial by Jury*, Sir Patrick Devlin (Stevens and Sons, London, 1966, first edition 1955), p. 130.

16. *Id.* at p. 130.

17. Forsyth, *op. cit.* at note 5, at p. 57.

18. Devlin, *op. cit.* at note 15, at p. 130.

19. Cornish, *op. cit.* at note 8, at p. 60.

20. "The Jury Abroad," anonymous, 221 The Law Times 118 (1956).

21. Cornish, *op. cit.* at note 8, at pp. 57-59.

22. Devlin, *op. cit.* at note 15, at p. 130.

23. Cornish, *op. cit.* at note 8, at p. 76.

24. Devlin, *op. cit.* at note 15, at p. 130.

25. *The Statues Revised*, 1933, C. 36.

26. *Watts* v. *Manning*, 2 All Eng. Rep. 267, 271 (1964).

27. Cornish, *op. cit.* at note 8, at p. 231.

28. Devlin, *op. cit.* at note 15, at p. 179.

29. Cornish, *op. cit.* at note 8, at p. 231j.

30. *Ibid.*

31. *The Evening News*, March 29, 1972, London, p. 1.

32. *Watts* v. *Manning*, 2 All Eng. Rep. 267, 269 (1964).

33. *Sims* v. *William Howard and Son Ltd.*, 1 All Eng. Rep. 918 (1964).

34. *Watts* v. *Manning*, 2 All Eng. Rep. 267, 272-73 (1964).

35. Devlin, *op. cit.* at note 15, at p. 180.

36. Cornish, *op. cit.* at note 8, at p. 76.

37. *The Statutes Revised*, 1870, C. 77, sec. 23.

38. Cornish, *op. cit.* at note 8, at p. 145.

39. *The Statutes Revised*, 1949, C. 27, sec. I(1).

40. *The Statutes Revised*, 1954, C. 41.

41. Cornish, *op. cit.* at note 8, at p. 53.

42. *The Statutes Revised*, 1825, C. 50.

43. Forsyth, *op. cit.* at note 5, at p. 232.

44. Forsyth, *op. cit.* at note 5, at p. 231.

45. Devlin, *op. cit.* at note 15, at p. 28.

46. *A History of English Law*, Sir William Holdsworth (Sweet and Maxwell, London, 1956 ed, 1st ed, 1903), I-327.

47. Forsyth, *op. cit.* at note 5, at p. 241.

48. *The Statutes Revised*, 1919, C. 71.

49. Cornish, *op. cit.* at note 8, at p. 28.

50. *The Statutes Revised*, 1931, C. 24.

51. *Public General Acts and Measures of 1965*, C. 26.

52. Cornish, *op. cit.* at note 8, at p. 162.

53. *The Proof of Guilt*, Glanville Williams (Stevens and Sons, London, 1963 ed., 1st ed. 1955), p. 130.

54. Cornish, *op. cit.* at note 8, at p. 162.

55. *Ibid.*

56. Williams, *op. cit.* at note 52, at pp. 303-04.

57. *Public General Acts and Measures,* 1967, C.80.

58. Cornish, *op. cit.* at note 8, at p. 68.

59. Holdsworth, *op. cit.* at note 45, at I-326.

60. Williams, *op. cit.* at note 52, at p. 45.

61. Williams, *op. cit.* at note 52, at pp. 11, 47, 71-72.

62. Cornish, *op. cit.* at note 8, at pp. 72-73.

63. Cornish, *op. cit.* at note 8, at p. 45.

64. Devlin, *op. cit.* at note 15, at p. 169.

65. Devlin, *op. cit.* at note 15, at p. 62.

66. Cornish, *op. cit.* at note 8, at p. 91.

67. Williams, *op. cit.* at note 52, at pp. 91-92.

68. Cornish, *op. cit.* at note 8, at p. 91.

69. Williams, *op. cit.* at note 52, at p. 72.

70. Devlin, *op. cit.* at note 15, at pp. 51-52, 54.

71. Williams, *op. cit.* at note 52, at pp. 101-04.

72. Devlin, *op. cit.* at note 16, at 166.

73. Cornish, *op. cit.* at note 8, at p. 10.

74. Devlin, *op. cit.* at note 15, at p. 166.

75. *The London Times,* March 7, 1972, p. 2.

76. *The Guardian,* February 14, 1972, p. 7.

77. "Early Opposition to the Petty Jury In Criminal Cases," Charles L. Wells, 30 Law Q. Rev. 97, 108 (1914).

78. Cornish, *op. cit.* at note 8, at pp. 245-46.

79. *Royal Mint Annual Report,* 1963, pp. 7-8.

80. *The Times* (London), January 24, 1973, p. 11.

81. *Ibid.*

82. *The Times* (London), February 14, 1973, p. 14.

83. *Ibid.*

X
The Constitutional Jury
(United States — 1800-1973)

As has been seen, the United States entered the nineteenth century with a burst of popular enthusiasm for the jury which that institution was never to receive again. Exactly what sort of jury was guaranteed by the constitutional passages previously quoted was still in the process of being determined by the courts in 1972. As far as the federal government was concerned, the jury had to consist of 12 members. This was decided by the case of *Thompson* v. *Utah*, 170 U.S. 343 (1898), in which the Supreme Court of the United States held that a federal jury must consist of 12 members. (The crime in this case occured in the territory of Utah before it became a state, where the defendant had been tried by a jury of eight after Utah had achieved statehood).

Generally, the number 12 was also adopted by the state courts except where another number was authorized by a constitutional provision.[1] The Fourteenth Amendment to the Constitution became effective on July 21, 1868, and it provided, in part, that:

> ...all persons born or naturalized in the United States, and subject to the jurisdiction thereof are citizens of the United States and of the State wherein they reside. No State shall make or enforce any law which shall abridge the privileges or immunities of citizens of the United States; nor shall any State deprive any person of life, liberty, or property, without due process of law; nor deny to any person within its jurisdiction the equal protection of the laws.[2]

This provision, however, was insufficient to require the state of Utah to comply with federal regulations concerning jury size, as was decided in the case of *Maxwell* v. *Dow*, 176 U.S. 581 (1900) where, at p. 603, the Supreme Court of the United States went so far as to offer the opinion that "Trial by jury has never been affirmed to be a necessary requisite of due process of law." Most state courts, however, kept to juries of 12 for serious criminal matters. As to lesser criminal charges and, occasionally, civil trials, it is not unusual to find state constitutions providing, as in Missouri, that juries may consist of less than 12 members.[3] New Mexico also provided that juries of six were sufficient in minor civil and criminal cases,[4] whereas it was decided in Alaska that juries could consist of from 6 to 12 members in courts not of record.[5]

Apparently, the question of the number of the members of the jury panel in serious criminal cases in state courts had not been laid to rest by the *Maxwell* decision, *supra,* and the Supreme Court of the United States considered the matter again in *Williams* v. *Florida,* 391 U.S. 78 (1970). The defendant in this case was convicted by a six man jury of robbery and sentenced to life imprisonment. In ruling that this jury did not violate the federal Constitution, Justice White, delivering the opinion of the court, at p. 102, said:

> We conclude, in short, as we began: the fact that the Jury at common law was composed of precisely 12 is a historical accident, unnecessary to effect the purposes [the main purpose according to the opinion of the court was to prevent oppression by the government] of the jury system and wholly without significance 'except to mystics.'

On June 21, 1973, Justice Brennan delivered the majority opinion in *Colgrove* v. *Battin,* ___ U.S. ___, 93 Sup. Ct., p. 2448, (June 21, 1973) which held that the local rule of the United States District Court for the District of Montana which provided for six member mini-juries did not violate the Seventh Amendment of the United States Constitution or the statute which authorized the promulgation of the federal rule of civil procedure (28 U.S.C.A. § 2072). The case also held that this rule was not inconsistent with provisions of the Federal Rules of Civil Procedure that authorize parties to stipulate to juries of less than 12 members. (Fed. Rules of Civ. Proc., rules 48, 83, 28 U.S.C.A.). Four members of the court dissented: Justices Marshall and Stewart on constitutional grounds as well as on the basis of statutory construction and their interpretation of the rules of civil procedure. Justices Douglas and Powell dissented only on the latter grounds. As of the date the opinion was delivered, rules providing for six-person juries in civil cases had been adopted in at least 55 federal district courts (*Colgrove* v. *Battin, supra,* 93 Sup. Ct. at p. 2449, fn. 1).

Justice Marshall noted that, "It is apparently uncontested that in 1791, common law civil juries consisted of 12 men." (*Colgrove* v. *Battin, supra,* 93 Sup.Ct. at p. 2460). He also said, "This six-man mutation is no more a jury than the panel of three judges condemned in *Baldwin* v. *New York,* 399 U.S. 66, 90 Sup. Ct. 1886, 26 L. Ed. 2d 437 (1970), or the 12 laymen instructed by a justice of the peace outlawed in *Capital Traction Co.* v. *Hof, supra.*" (*Colgrove* v. *Battin, supra,* 93 Sup. Ct. at p. 2458). There can be no scholarly answer to Justice Marshall's historically based opinion other than the "mystic" preponderance of "five" over "four".

Perhaps the court was right, but it is doubtful that the opinion would be shared by America's numerous minorities who had their chances of being represented on a criminal jury reduced in half by this decision. One of the functions of a reasonably large size is to insure that various elements of the community are represented — not only members of the dominant majority. Neither can it be assumed that a group of six functions in the same way as a group of 12 in arriving at a decision. A group of six is more nearly the size of the usual club committee that habitually operates on the basis of consensus. The larger membership of 12 is more akin to the entire group where it is more usual to hear conflicting opinions. A single personality can occasionally impress his will on 12 jurors, but an aggressive personality is more likely to meet stronger opposition from a larger group of jurors.

The basis for public respect for the jury has been precisely because matters of great importance have traditionally been submitted to a body of 12 members. All societies that have endured have, consciously or otherwise, emphasized the authority of their institutions by appealing to the antiquity of their forms. Of course, one of the original reasons for the large number was to have a decision immediately supported by a significant body, namely, the members of the jury themselves. Halving the jury is therefore a disadvantage, although it decreases the likelihood of a hung jury, and thus increases the chances of conviction. Lowering the number of jurors raises the quantum of proof* necessary for an acquittal, and lessens the authority and respect that the jury possesses. Although this line of reasoning is based on the more emotional or "mystical" aspects of man, mysticism itself is in many ways at the root of submission to authority, and should not be ignored if those institutions are to continue to be strong.

When Forsyth was writing in 1852, he could realistically say that the principle of unanimity was generally upheld in the United States in civil and criminal trials.[6] In the federal courts, this principle has never been questioned in civil or criminal cases, although in the state courts it is another matter. It was estimated in 1968 that, in civil matters, 18 states provide for a majority verdict of one sort or another.[7] The constitution of Ohio permits civil juries to return verdicts when nine out of 12 agree,[8] and Alaska, Hawaii, Idaho, Nevada, South Dakota and Washington have similar provisions.[9] Minnesota provides that five-sixths may return a verdict in civil matters if no agreement is reached in six hours,[10] while New Jersey, Michigan and New York also provide for verdicts in civil cases by five-sixths vote.[11] Missouri's constitution provides for a verdict by two-thirds in civil and criminal courts not of record. In civil cases in courts of record, the Missouri constitution provides for verdicts by three-fourths.[12] In Montana, all civil juries and all misdemeanor criminal juries render verdicts by two-thirds vote.[13] Oregon's constitution permits criminal juries to render a verdict upon the agreement of 10 unless a capital case is being tried.[14]

Perhaps it goes without saying that it is essential to due process that the jury be impartial.[15] Pennsylvania took no chances, providing by their constituion for "...an impartial jury of

---

* The phrase "quantum of proof" is not used as the equivalent of "burden of proof," but is merely used to indicate the various factors involved in jury decisions.

the vincinage."[16] Most lawyers would not think of trying a jury case without a judge to preside, but it has been attempted, although such a trial is not a constitutional jury under the federal law.[17] It was not until 1930 in the case of *Patton* v. *United States*, 281 U.S. 276 (1930), that it was definitely decided that a criminal defendant in the federal system could waive trial by jury. As to state courts, a jury was waived in Maryland as early as 1829, while Maryland provided by statute that the jury could be waived in all cases in 1852.[18] Wisconsin provided for the jury to be waived by the consent of both parties in 1848.[19] In Michigan's 1964 constitution, it was provided, in a not unusual provision, that a jury was automatically waived in civil cases.[20]

As late as 1968, the United States Supreme Court decided that the constitutional right to a jury extended to charges of contempt. In the case of *Bloom* v. *Illinois*, 391 U.S. 194 (1968), at 198, it was held:

> Our deliberations have convinced us, however, that serious contempts are so nearly like other serious crimes that they are subject to the jury trial provision of the Constitution, now binding on the States, and that the tradition is constitutionally infirm as it permits other than petty contempts to be tried without honoring a demand for a jury trial.

The Fifth Amendment to the United States Constitution has preserved the grand jury on a federal level, but the due process clause has not yet been extended to the state grand jury. It was held in *Hurtado* v. *People*, 110 U.S. 516 (1889), that the "...'due process' clause of the Fourteenth Amendment does not require indictment by grand jury in prosecution for murder." Sometimes other duties in addition to considering criminal accusations are given to the grand jury. The consitituion of Alaska (1959), for example, provides that the grand jurors may make recommendations for the public welfare.[21]

Of course, there are many cases that are not constitutionally required to be tried by a jury. It is common knowledge that divorce and equity cases are tried to the court alone in the United States. In federal courts, a defendant can be tried by a judge without a jury and imprisoned for up to 90 days.[22] Louisiana, Utah and Colorado do not have constitutional guarantees for jury trial in civil matters,[23] while in New York, as a practical matter in criminal cases, trial by jury is limited to felonies.[24] In civil cases it is often provided that minimum dollar amounts must be in controversy before a jury trial is possible. Some of these amounts include twenty dollars in federal courts, $250 in Alaska, $500 in New Hampshire, and $100 in Hawaii.[25] In many states, it has also been decided that juveniles should be tried for all charges (criminal in nature although perhaps not styled in that way) without a jury.[26] The constitution of Texas, in a fairly typical provision, permits commitment up to 90 days without a jury on charges of mental incapacity.[27]

But, it is not court trials which threaten the position of the jury. It is more likely that concepts such as "no-fault" insurance will do more to diminish the frequency of trials by jury in civil matters than any other concept. This, if it occurs, will be unfortunate. Jury trials may become infrequent and, in civil cases, relegated to comparatively unimportant disputes. Lawyers are aware of the tendency of boards and arbitrators to adopt rigid standards, particularly as to damages for injuries. The English experience discussed previously is an example of this, as are the boards which make awards for industrial injuries in the United States. Desirable as it is to expedite the payment of compensation even in those cases where the victim may be at fault, the victim, if the amount is substantial, should always have the option to elect to have a jury fix the damages. This is not just to protect the individual but the public generally by having at least occasional jury verdicts for reference so that the system will not become rigid. Also, the public will continue to have the habit of trial by jury, and the criminal jury will be a more acceptable mode of trial then it would be if only criminal cases were tried to juries.

The jury has still retained its strength in criminal matters, and a verdict of acquittal is still conclusive.[28] Although it has not been clearly established if the state courts can abolish the civil jury, it has been decided that they cannot abolish the criminal jury when the charge is serious. In the case of *Duncan* v. *Loui-*

---

siana, 391 U.S. 145 (1968), the defendant had been tried by a judge despite his request for a jury. He was faced with a possible fine of $300 and up to two years in jail if convicted. The judge found him guilty and sentenced him to 60 days in the parish prison and fined him $150. Justice White, in the strongest judicial defense of the jury in modern times, wrote the majority opinion. Before tracing the history and importance of the jury, he stated the holding of the court, at page 149:

> Because we believe that trial by jury in criminal cases is fundamental to the American scheme of justice, we hold that the Fourteenth Amendment guarantees a right of jury trial in all criminal cases which — were they to be tried in a federal court — would come within the Sixth Amendment's guarantee.

There are, in addition, some interesting miscellaneous provisions concerning the status of the jury during its development in the United States. For example, a statute of New York in 1801 provided that the bailiff in charge of a jury would keep the jury without meat or drink except water.[29] This, however, was an anomaly and was not a continuing or general problem. Missouri was the only slave state to provide a jury trial for slaves charged with crime.[30] New Hampshire, before 1852, was an early leader in providing that jurors be compensated for their time and expense.[31] Wigmore says that a jury member can still be called as a witness and that after testifying he returns to the jury box.[32] A Georgia statute allows the jurors to take notes.[33] In an important holding, Judge Holmes seemed to indicate that a jury verdict might sometimes have the effect of *stare decisis*. With reference to a previous verdict which established that the conduct in question was comprised within an anti-gambling statute, he said, "...it is not necessary to go on forever, taking the opinion of the jury in each new case that comes up."[34]

Panaceas for jury ills such as pretrial, split trials and court appointed witnesses, seem not to have been popularly received.[35] In 20 states, instructions by the court precedes argument by counsel.[36] Cornish claims that United States juries have unreasonably refused to convict in drunk driving cases, game violations, bootlegging and moonshining. He notes that well publicized awards have a noticeable effect on following juries. In addition, Cornish observes that the "white" majority in the United States has freely expressed its prejudices while serving on juries.[37] There is no doubt a higher percentage of acquittals in the cases Cornish listed, but that should not necessarily be assumed to be a defect of the jury. There have also been many convictions, and, in other cases, the juries, under the facts of particular cases, have chosen to "pardon" the defendants rather than ruin their lives. As to the publicity effect, it is certainly arguable that verdicts are far from being too high. It is the reverse of the criticism of the English who say that the jury doesn't know what the other verdicts are. As far as prejudice on juries is concerned, where blacks are systematically eliminated from jury service, this cannot even be termed a "jury" in a real sense. There should be a determined effort to obtain minority representation by insuring that all substantial minorities are included in the *venire* with a reasonable chance of sitting on the trial jury. This could be insured by keeping the jury's number at 12. The minority should be made effective by keeping the rule of unanimity in civil and criminal cases.

In the air of pristine democracy that existed at the beginning of the nineteenth century, juries, both civil and criminal on all levels of government, had the right to judge law as well as fact. The right to judge law was never as firmly entrenched in civil as in criminal cases.[38] John C. Spencer, an American attorney, expressed his opinion in notes to the American edition of *Democracy In America*, by DeTocqueville, that:

> In cases at common law, there are questions of fact and questions of law — the former are invariably tried by a jury, the latter, whether presented in the course of a jury trial, or by pleading, in which the facts are admitted, are always decided by the judges.[39]

Mainly because of the court's power in civil cases to order a new trial if the jury finds against the direction of the court, the jury's right in civil cases was never comparable to their irreversable right in criminal cases.[40] Wigmore wrote in the twentieth century:

The doctrine has obtained in a few jurisdictions that the jury, in dealing with the local law applicable to the case, has in criminal cases a legal right to repudiate the instructions of the judge and to determine the law for themselves. But this ill-advised doctrine, defiant of the fundamentals of law, had only narrow acceptance.[41]

Wigmore was wrong when he said that the doctrine had only narrow acceptance and when he implied that the right was limited to criminal cases, but he was right to the extent that he implied the doctrine had little acceptance at the time he was writing. There still exists, however, some narrow areas in which the jury has the right as well as the power to judge law.

A decision by Justice Story was the first federal judge to cast doubt on the jury's right to decide law.[42] The jury's right was finally denied in the federal courts in *Sparf and Hansen* v. *United States,* 156 U.S. 51 (1895). The court, at page 102, held, "We must hold firmly to the doctrine that in the courts of the United States it is the duty of juries in criminal cases to take the law from the court and apply that law to the facts as they find them to be from the evidence." But, at page 105 he continues, "...it is not competent for the court, in a criminal case, to instruct the jury peremptorily to find the accused guilty of the offense charged or of any criminal offense less than that charged." The right was gone, but the power remained.

In the state courts, New York's Court of Appeals split on the question in 1804,[43] and finally denied the right in 1863.[44] A Massachusetts attorney risked contempt by arguing law contrary to the direction of the court in 1808, and by doing so he obtained an acquittal for his client. The same year, the jury was given the right by statute to decide law as well as fact, but the jurors had the option to return a special verdict for a general verdict subject to the opinion of the court on a point stated. This statute was repealed in 1836, but it was held permissible for a lawyer to argue law contrary to the direction of the court in 1847, although the jury was charged to take its law from the court. A statute gave the jury the power to decide law in criminal cases in 1855, but, despite this statute, the supreme court of the state held that law was for the judge to decide.[45]

Pursuant to statutory rule-making authority, the Supreme Court of Connecticut made it a rule for the courts to declare their opinion of the law of the case to the jury. Another statute to the same effect was enacted in 1812, covering civil and criminal cases. Blunting this trend was an 1821 statute of that state which required the court to direct the jury on the law in civil cases but to only state the court's opinion in criminal cases. The jury, in criminal cases, was to consider both law and fact. The Supreme Court of Connecticut, 81 years later, held that, notwithstanding this statute, the jury must accept its law from the court. A statute buttressed this position in 1918.[46]

In early Illinois, the juries judged both fact and law, and this right was given by an 1822 statute. Until 1931 it was thought to be the law of the state that a lawyer could argue law to the jury.[47] New Hampshire had this right until 1843,[48] but Tennessee was unclear on the issue until 1852, when it was held that the court was the only witness to the law. The right to decide law in Tennessee was finally lost in 1881.[49] Maine had the right in 1860,[50] but later lost it,[51] and Vermont lost the right in 1897.[52] It appears that Pennsylvania did not clearly lose the right until 1923;[53] Rhode Island had the right initially but lost it by 1860.[54] The right was denied in Maryland in 1804, but even after the constitutional grant to the jury of the right to decide law and fact, the court still denied the jury the right to rule on the constitutionality of a statute.[55] Before 1860, the jury's right to decide law had been denied in Alabama, Kentucky, Mississippi, Missouri, North Carolina, Ohio and Texas.[56] Virginia did not reject the right until 1881.[57]

Indiana denied the right in 1828, allowed it in 1830, denied it in 1851 and established it by constitutional provision in 1858.[58] Louisiana had the right by statute in the beginning, lost it in 1871 and obtained it in 1879 by this constitutional amendment: "...the jury in all criminal cases shall be the judges of the law and of the facts on the question of guilt or innocence, having been charged as to the law applicable to the case by the presiding judge." However, this provision notwithstanding, it was held in 1885 that Louisiana juries had to take the law from the judges.[59]

A Georgia statute of 1833 said that juries were to be judges of fact and law and were, in every case, to deliver a general verdict of guilty or not guilty. It was held in 1861 that the jury had to take its law from the judge, and this continued to be the law regardless of a constitutional provision of 1877 which purported to make the jury the judge of law and fact.[60] It is still provided in the Georgia constitution as follows:

> In all prosecutions or indictments for libel the truth may be given in evidence; and the jury in all criminal cases shall be the judges of the law and facts. The power of the judges to grant new trials in case of conviction is preserved.[61]

The constitution of Missouri still contains the passage, "...and suits and prosecutions for libel the jury, under the direction of the court shall determine the law and the facts."[62] Still, it is said that the right of the jury to decide law has been repudiated in all states except Indiana and Maryland.[63]

The impact of the jury process, from the point of view of size alone, is considerable. There are approximately 60,000 criminal jury trials in the United States every year and another 20,-000 that are not carried to a verdict.[64] In the rest of the world, there are about 10,000 jury trials a year with England and Wales accounting for half of that number.[65] Also, in the United States there is a great diversity between states. Connecticut has three criminal jury trials a year per 100,000 persons of population and Georgia has 144, while the national average is 35.[66] In 1945, of all criminal felony charges, 75 percent of those charged pleaded guilty, 10 percent were tried to the bench and 15 percent were tried to a jury.[67] One seventh of all felony prosecutions end in a jury trial. The percentage of judge trials and guilty pleas is higher for misdemeanors.[68]

In 1973, we find the jury is apparently well entrenched as a matter of right in criminal cases. This is primarily due to the substantial protection that the right to jury has received from the United States Supreme Court. The civil jury is generally very much alive, with two or three states excepted, but is subject to continuing criticism. The value of the jury to modern society in the United States will be our final consideration.

Chapter X Footnotes

1. "Trial by Jury and The Reform of Civil Procedure," Austin Wakeman, 31 Harv. L. Rev. 669, 673 (1918).

2. *Federal Code Annotated,* Constitution volume, (Bobbs-Merrill Co., 1950), p. 29.

3. *Constitutions of the United States, National and State,* For Legislative Research Fund of Columbia University (Dobbs-Terry, N.Y.).

4. *Ibid.*

5. *Ibid.*

6. *History of Trial by Jury,* William Forsyth (John W. Parker and Son, London, 1852), p. 344.

7. "With Love In Their Hearts But Reform on Their Minds," 4 Col. J. of L. and Soc. Pro. 178, 193 (1968).

8. Constitutions...,*op. cit.* at note 3.

9. *Id.* at appropriate constitution.

10. *Id.* at Minnesota constitutions.

11. *Id.* at appropriate constitution.

12. *Id.* at Missouri constitution.

13. *Id.* at Montana constitution.

14. *Id.* at Oregon constitution.

15. "Trial by Jury...," *op. cit.* at note 1, at pp. 674-75.

16. Constitutions..., *op. cit.* at note 3, at Pennsylvania constitution.

17. *Capital Traction* v. *Hof,* 174 U.S. 1 (1899).

18. *The American Jury,* Harry Kalven, Jr. and Hans Zeisel (Little, Brown and Company, Boston, 1966), p. 22.

19. Forsyth, *op. cit.* at note 6, at p. 344.

20. Constitutions..., *op. cit.* at note 3, at Michigan constitution.

21. Constitutions..., *op. cit.* at note 3, at Alaska constitution.

22. "Can a State Abolish The Civil Jury?" Delmar Karlen, Wis. L. Rev. (1965) p. 103, at p. 107.

23. "Abolition of the Civil Jury," Bruce Rashkow, 15 DePaul L. Rev. 416, 417 (1965).

24. Karlen, *op. cit.* at note 22, at p. 111.

25. *Federal Code Annotated, op. cit.* at note 2, at p. 28, Seventh Amendment, United States Constitution; and *Constitutions...,* at note 3, at appropriate state constitution.

26. Karlen, *op. cit.* at note 22, at p. 108.

27. Constitutions..., *op. cit.* at note 3, at Texas constitution.

28. *Courts on Trial,* Jerome Frank (Princeton Univ. Press, Princeton, N.J., 1949), p. 112.

29. *Capital Traction* v. *U.S.,* 174 U.S. 1, (1899), at pp. 34-35.

30. Forsyth, *op. cit.* at note 6, at p. 344.

31. *Ibid.*

32. *Wigmore on Evidence,* Wigmore (Little, Brown and Co., Boston), VI-594.

33. "The Functions of The Jury," Dale W. Broeder, 21 Univ. Chi. L. Rev. 386, 392 (1954).

34. *Commonwealth* v. *Sullivan,* 146 Mass. 142, 15 N.E. 491, 494 (1888).

35. "With Love In Their Hearts...," *op. cit.* at note 7, at p. 194.

36. *The Jury,* W.R. Cornish (The Penguin Press, London, 1968), p. 115.

37. *Id.* at pp. 119-20, 141, 292.

38. "Juries as Judges of the Criminal Law," Mark DeWolfe Howe, 52 Harv. L. Rev. 582, 589 (1939).

39. *Democracy In America,* Alexis Clerel DeTocqueville, translated by Henry Reeves, Esq., with preface and notes by John C. Spencer (George Adlard, New York, 3rd Am. Ed, 1839, 1st Am. Ed. 1838), p. 280.

40. *Reports of Cases Argued In the Superior Court of Judicature of the Province of Massachusetts Bay, Between 1761-1772,* Josiah Quincy, Jr. (Little, Brown, and Co., Boston, 1865), p. 567.

41. Wigmore, *op. cit.* at note 32, at IX-530.

42. Howe, *op. cit.* at note 37, at pp. 589-90.

43. Quincy, *op. cit.* at note 39, at p. 568.

44. Howe, *op. cit.* at note 38, at p. 596.

45. Howe, *op. cit.* at note 38, at pp. 605-10.

46. Howe, *op. cit.* at note 38, at pp. 601-02.

47. Howe, *op. cit.* at note 38, at pp. 610-11.

48. Quincy, *op. cit.* at note 40, at p. 568.

49. Howe, *op. cit.* at note 38, at pp. 598-99.

50. Quincy, *op. cit.* at note 40, at p. 568.

51. Howe, *op. cit.* at note 38, at p. 496.

52. Howe, *op. cit.* at note 38, at p. 593.

53. Howe, *op. cit.* at note 38, at p. 595.

54. Quincy, *op. cit.* at note 40, at p. 568.

55. Quincy, *op. cit.* at note 40, at p. 569.

56. Quincy, *op. cit.* at note 40, at pp. 569-70.

57. Howe, *op. cit.* at note 38, at p. 597.

58. Quincy, *op. cit.* at note 40, at p. 569-70.

59. Howe, *op. cit.* at note 38, at p. 597.

60. Howe, *op. cit.* at note 38, aT p. 598.

61. Constitutions..., *op. cit.* at note 3, at Georgia constitution.

62. Constitutions..., *op. cit.* at note 3, at Missouri constitution.

63. Broeder, *op. cit.* at note 33, at p. 403.

64. Kalven and Zeisel, *op. cit.* at note 18, at p. 12.

65. Kalven and Zeisel, *op. cit.* at note 18, at p. 13.

66. Kalven and Zeisel, *op. cit.* at note 18, at p. 16.

67. Kalven and Zeisel, *op. cit.* at note 18, at p. 18.

68. Kalven and Zeisel, *op. cit.* at note 18, at p. 17.

Chapter XI
The Summing Up

In an age when all things are subject to question, we should not be surprised to find that "... the market has turned against trial by jury."[1] Yet, considering the ancient origins of the jury, it seems only yesterday that legal opinion considered the jury to be the *sine qua non* for the trial of serious matters. Shortly before the turn of the century, Joseph H. Choate, in an address to the American Bar Association, could say with confidence, despite Mark Twain,* that:

> The truth is, however, that the jury system is so fixed as an essential part of our political institution... that there can be no substantial ground for fear that any of us will live to see the people consent to give it up.[2]

It is puzzling to watch the recent United States Supreme Court decisions which have transformed the concept of trial by jury into something entirely different than its original meaning, considering the extent of the respect that it held throughout United States history. As a matter of fact, as late as 1892 the English Parliament had reconfirmed the importance of the jury 58 times,[3] while in 1968 the U.S. Supreme Court ruled that jury trial was a constitutional right in state courts in serious criminal trials.[4]

The same court held in 1970, however, that:

> ... the fact that the common law jury was composed of twelve is a historical accident, unnecessary to effect the purpose of the jury system and wholly without significance 'except to mystics.'[5]

The latest case in this series, *Johnson* v. *Louisiana*, 406 U.S. 356, 92 S.Ct. 1620 (1972), ruled that a criminal jury need not be unanimous. The last two cases also dealt with the constitutional requirements of jury trial in state courts. The holdings of the court in all three cases were expressed in opinions by Justice White.

---

* "The jury system puts a ban upon intelligence and honesty, and a premium upon ignorance, stupidity, and perjury. It is a shame that we must continue to use a worthless system because it *was* good a thousand years ago." *Roughing It*, Mark Twain (Limited Editions Club, New York, 1972, 1st printed Jan. 30, 1872), p. 247. Emphasis that of Mark Twain.

Justice Thurgood Marshall was understandably puzzled by the court's failure to maintain the principle of unanimity and a membership of 12 — features which had been central to jury trials for hundreds of years. He said:

> We are asked to decide what is the nature of the 'jury' that is guaranteed by the Sixth Amendment. I would have thought that history provided the appropriate guide...[6]

Justice Marshall had good reason to be concerned about the future of the jury. On January 1, 1971, less than two years after the Supreme Court had held that the number 12 was a historical accident, the Federal District Court of Minnesota adopted a rule that juries in civil cases would consist of six jurors. By June of 1972, more than 40 of the other 92 district courts had adopted similar rules.[7] All of this was apparently based on the authority of *Williams, supra.*

Opinions which denigrate the value of jury trial are not a new phenomenon. Justice Cardozo lent respectability to modern criticism of trial by jury when he said, in *Connecticut* v. *U.S.*, 302 U.S. 319, 325 (1939):

> The right to trial by jury and the immunity to prosecution except as the result of an indictment may have value and importance. Even so, they are not of the very essence of a scheme of ordered liberty.

Perhaps the leading modern critic of trial by jury is Jerome Frank. He said:

> I submit that the jury is the worst possible enemy of that ideal of the 'supremacy of law.' For jury-made law is par excellence, capricious and arbitrary, yielding to the maximum in way of lack of uniformity, and of unknowability.[8]

More forceful yet is the criticism of Leon Sarky:

> Related to present day American life, civil jury trials represent the horse and buggy segment of American administration of justice, reflecting a judicial provincialism and a mid-Victorian drag on our judicial proc-

ess, which calls for realistic treatment by way of reform.[9]

Balancing these adverse opinions is Thomas Jefferson who
was not bashful in his defense of the jury:

> Were I called upon to decide, whether the people had
> best be omitted in the legislative or judicial depart-
> ment, I would say it is better to leave them out of the
> legislative. The execution of the laws is more impor-
> tant than the making of them.[10]

Justice White, when he wrote the opinion in *Duncan* v. *Louisiana*,
391 U.S. 145, 155 (1968), appeared to be a staunch friend of the
jury. He said:

> Providing an accused with the right to be tried by a
> jury of his peers gave him inestimable safeguard
> against the corrupt or overzealous prosecutor and
> against the compliant, biased, or eccentric judge.

Judges, the chief competition to the jury, have also been
criticized, as the following samples will show. Jeremy Bentham's
opinion of the judiciary (which, except at the lowest levels, is
filled exclusively from the bar in England) is clear:

> Filling the bench from no other fund than the bar, is it
> not exactly such a mode as if boarding-school-mis-
> tresses and governesses, were never to be chosen but
> from brothels?[11]

Less vehement but also expressing dissatisfaction with the
judiciary was Charles Grove Haines:

> The morality of courts may be higher than the moral-
> ity of traders or of politicians, but it has, of course, of-
> ten happened that the ideas entertained by the judges
> have fallen below the highest and most enlightened
> public opinion of a particular time.[12]

There can be no consensus as to the relative merits of a
judge or jury trial, or, for that matter, other modes of trial. It is
obviously impractical to sequester the critics in a room apart
without food or drink until they come to a unanimous decision,
and each juror will continue to be guided in large part by his

own personal experience. Still, observations and analysis based on the authorities and the writer's experience in over 150 jury trials might well prove stimulating to those who are concerned with the preservation of trial by jury. It ought to be noted, however, that the writer is solidly of the opinion that trial by jury ought to be preserved with the common law features it possessed at the time of the adoption of the United States Constitution. Improvements will be suggested, but they will not relate to the essential features of the jury, such as the number of the jurors or unanimity of the verdict. In fact, the danger of even small changes was foreseen by Blackstone who wrote with reference to changes in the jury system:

> ... though began in trifles, the precedent may gradually increase and spread to the utter disuse of juries in questions of the most momentous concern.[13]

The rapid adoption of the minijuries is an apparent confirmation of Blackstone's fears.

There are certain disadvantages in trial by a judge alone as compared to trial by jury, which can be demonstrated by an examination of the respective modes of trial apart from historical considerations. The disadvantages of a judge trial are due to the inherent features of this trial as compared to jury trial; for example, (1) the judge's period of service is long, while the jury's is short; (2) the judge can rule only by himself, whereas the jury has the added fairness of more members; (3) the identity of the judge is well known long in advance of trial, whereas the identity of jurors is learned shortly before trial; and (4) judges can be removed on motion of a client only upon demonstrating prejudice, while at least some jurors can be challenged without showing cause.

The judge's long tenure and wide acquaintance cause him to become suspected of favoritism regardless of his actions. It is often noted by members of the bar, and even by litigants themselves, that judges socialize with the members of the legal profession, and more often than not with only the most successful members. This is natural, though, and not the result of an evil plan to subvert justice.

It is common for a lawyer to be asked by clients, "Is there any way to get to the judge?" When it is explained that it is a criminal offense to try such an action, the clients have been known to say, "I didn't mean we would bribe him, but perhaps there is another lawyer who could help out who is close to the judge." After the case is tried, if the decision were unfavorable, the clients will always suspect the judge of favoritism or dishonesty, and all the explanation in the world to the contrary falls on deaf ears. (If the decision were patently stupid, however, as occasionally happens, the lawyer himself cannot avoid secret imagination on the subject.)

On the other hand, litigants seldom suspect the jury, as they were picked by lot, investigated thoroughly and were subject to challenge. A client may say, "I was disappointed in Jones. I felt sure he would side with us," but he seldom suspects the entire jury of outright dishonesty. Even if he does believe the jury has been corrupted, he does not feel it would be futile to venture into court again, as he would have a new jury. Judges tend to hold office perpetually and, therefore, despite the honesty of a particular judge, a percentage of the people will inevitably come to believe that certain lawyers and interests obtain better results before one judge than others. This is not to say, of course, that there are no dishonest judges, even on the much admired English bench.[14] Part of the problem with judges is inherent in the fact that a law suit almost always produces a loser and a winner. When parties decide to go to court, they both believe that they have at least some portion of right on their side. To the extent that they lose this right, it does little to ease the hurt to be told the injustice was according to law.

The accumulation of frustration affects lawyers as well as clients. The writer has overheard a lawyer say, "I've never won a case tried before Judge N.T. sitting without a jury." This was a prosperous lawyer who had a large office practice, but who only occasionally ventured into court. His luck with the judge had been disastrous. His luck had not been altogether good with juries, but there he was consoled by the thought that there would be a new jury next time.

One lawyer in a southern Ohio county once won 15 jury

cases in a row, both civil and criminal. If this had been accomplished before a judge, there would have been strong suspicion of corruption. It is just possible that the clients of this lawyer deserved to win all those cases; the jurors don't know the lawyers' specific record in this regard, but the judges do. Lawyers therefore suspect judges of compensating in one case for what a lawyer lost in a previous one. Jurors are not given this opportunity to trade justice, however, due to their short tenure.

Observation as a practicing lawyer provides more substantial evidence that some judges do not always conduct themselves according to the rules. For example, more than one judge has been known to attend legal seminars at the expense of counsel who practice before them. Generally the misconduct of lawyers and judges themselves must be flagrant before it will be subject to punishment in magistrates' courts, and this is particularly true with regard to violations relating to alcohol and automobiles.

This protection even extends to those associated with the bar. The writer once went to court with a distant relative who was charged with operating a motor vehicle under the influence of alcohol. Both parties had a valid case, and so a plea to reckless driving was accepted. After the hearing, the judge discovered that the client was a relative of mine and asked, "Why didn't you say something?" There was a clear implication that the relationship entitled the client to a different brand of justice. Judges have little compunction about levying heavy fines on persons with no community or political leverage, but hesitate to "ruin" the career of a doctor or lawyer with a compulsory sentence of three days in jail for drunken driving. These same judges will criticize a jury that acquits an industrial worker of the exact charge.

Although a particular jury cannot continue its peculiar brand of injustice over a period of years, judges, consciously or unconsciously, have a way of trading in on judicial favors at election time. The writer has seldom met a judge of a magistrates court who was not guilty, at least unconsciously, of using his office for personal patronage by dispensing favors. A part of the problem seems to be that no matter how honest and careful the judge may be, he cannot avoid the suspicion of professional misconduct if he remains in office over a period of years.

An English barrister was heard extolling the virtues of the English judiciary who try most civil cases without juries. The writer asked him, "If the judges are so capable, why don't judges try all criminal cases without juries? After all, the very best tribunal ought to be used in cases of the highest importance where life and reputation are at stake." The barrister, surprisingly, said that judges sitting alone did not constitute a better tribunal for ascertaining truth than the jury, but only a more convenient tribunal. For the most serious matters he still preferred the jury. He was supported by no less an authority than Lord Denning who said, in 1967, that he still preferred juries for serious crimes, and that the jury was still "...one of the pillars of our freedom."[15] One cannot help but feel, however, that some seemingly insignificant matters nonetheless could have a great impact on an individual's life. As Shakespeare's Shylock said:

> Nay, take my life and all; pardon not that:
> You take my house, when you do take the prop
> that doth sustain my house; you take my life,
> When you do take the means whereby I live. (IV.1.375)

Custody of children, invariably tried by judges in the United States, and damages in serious personal injury cases are only two common examples of civil litigation involving issues of the utmost importance. The argument that only criminal cases are important enough to justify the trouble of a jury trial is a specious argument found in the mouths of those who are not friendly to jury trial. This recalls what Repp said in 1832:

> Whatever some learned Judges may say in commendation of juries in their books, it would be difficult to find one friendly to that institution in practice, unless he happened to have Juries so well trained, that they conscientiously attend to every hint from the bench.[16]

Apart from real or imagined bias on the part of judges, it is thought by some authorities that the professionalism of the law is a lifetime process of degeneration into insensibility leaving judges unfit to solve the endless variety of disputes that come to the courts for resolution. Forsyth suggested that juries act as a check upon the "narrow subtlety" to which professional lawyers are subject.[17] In describing a judge trial without a jury, Holdsworth said, "One finds oneself in a rarified atmosphere of morality and respectability in which life is hardly possible."[18]

Devlin expressed this professional failing by saying, "The malady that sooner or later affects most men of a profession is that they tend to construct a mistique that cuts them off from common man."[19]

The novelist, George Eliot, also diagnosed this ailment through the lips of Lydgate in *Middlemarch*. "In my opinion..., legal training only makes a man more incompetent in questions that require knowledge of another kind."[20]

As contrasted with the judge, the jury is alleged to be the depository of common sense. The types of cases appearing in court are as various as the backgrounds of the litigants. No single individual can be expected to view every case in court from the necessary points of view in order to properly understand it — no matter how much learning and good intentions he possesses. As Devlin said:

> I think it must be agreed that there are some determinations in which twelve minds are better than one, however skilled, and most people would accept that the determination whether a witness is telling the truth is one of them.[21]

A common practice is to base legal seminars on the theory that a lawyer is not capable of trying a particular lawsuit unless he has the specialized knowledge of a surgeon, a civil engineer, or a criminologist, as the case may require. Lawyers forget that at the basis of their knowledge should be an understanding of human nature. Lawyers must understand the witness to be able to examine him, while the technical knowledge for each trial can be learned or reviewed for each case. The tools acquired and retained by the lawyer during the course of his life enable him to handle the over confident braggart, elicit believable truth from the introvert and bring down to earth the fantasy of a child. The lawyer must be able to extract from the evidence the essence of credibility and redeliver it during summation, using all his understanding of human nature and the art of persuasion.

The same persons who would reduce the personal injury lawyer to a medical technician would reduce the trial of injury cases to administrative procedures before a board of doctors, a process more out of touch with the human elements involved than judges are now. In short, judges, like all professionals, are apt to develop early "hardening of the categories,"[22] finding a category for a case whether it fits or not, while juries subordinate law to justice.[23]

Judges are considered to be subjected to more extra-judicial influence than juries. The most common example of this influence is the readiness of magistrates to accept police evidence. Williams insists that the jury is right to be slower than the judge in accepting the word of an officer against a defendant.[24] Cornish observed that those who regularly appeared in magistrates courts were aware of the tendency to accept police evidence "without demur,"[25] and the danger is apparent when the judge claims, "I've heard that story before," although it is possible that the defendant may be innocent.[26] In one case, an English detective caused a series of unfounded prosecutions to be launched, although eventually he was found to be mentally ill.[27] No class of witnesses is so bound to the truth as to be worthy of belief in every instance, and juries are more cognizant of this than judges.

The jury was recognized by Forsyth as being a bulwark against arbitrary action on the part of the crown.[28] Devlin says that history shows that the executive branch of government has been more successful in finding judges who will bend to its will than it has been in finding juries with such amenable backbones.[29] Holdsworth touched on a different aspect of the same problem when he noted that juries kept the law in touch "with life."[30]

When De Tocqueville visited America in 1831, it may have been that juries, far from being a cause of court congestion, expedited justice. At least that was the opinion of John C. Spencer, an American lawyer who wrote the preface and notes to the American edition to De Tocqueville's *Democracy In America* which was first published in 1838. Spencer wrote, "By introducing the jury into the business of the courts you are enabled to diminish the number of judges; which is a very great advantage."[31]

Now, though, it is common for authorities to blame juries for the law's delay.

One authority, writing in 1962-63, said it took five and one-half years for jury trials to be tried in Nassau County in New York, while cases tried to judges sitting alone in Louisiana were tried within six months of a request for trial.[32] Cornish says that, "... trial by jury is a cumbersome and expensive method of trying a case; at the very least, this places the onus of proving its value on those who wish to see it continue."[33]

He also claims judges work faster than juries.[34] Another authority claims jury trials are 60 percent longer than court trials.[35] Kalven and Zeisel note that juries cause delays in civil litigation and constitute an unfair tax on the time of underpaid jurors.[36]

Other authorities, however, claim jury trials take very little longer than judge trials if other factors not considered by other studies are taken into account.[37] These factors include the time it takes for a judge to deliberate and write his opinion. A study to determine the effect of the abolition of juries would result in the saving of the time of 1.6 judges out of a total of 26.[38] In fact, it is possible that there would be no saving of time when all the factors are considered.[39] On one occasion, for example, counsel had agreed to waive a jury and try a matter under the federal wage and hour law to the court. After the evidence was in and the case had been submitted, some weeks passed and no decision was forthcoming, and so, upon prompting of clients, inquiry was made and the judge replied that he would render a decision shortly. There were many inquiries and many promises. After about a year, the judge said he had decided to step aside and ask another judge to hear the case. This meant starting over.

In another case involving the title to a public cemetery, the case was argued and submitted. The court requested the reporter to prepare a transcript. Counsel also obtained copies to use in preparing briefs. The briefs were submitted and months passed. Inquiry was made by letter and phone over a period of months. The judge told counsel that he had been busy and that this case was next on his list. Nothing was said about a transcript in reply to any inquiries. More time elapsed, and one of the parties resorted to self-help which received wide newspaper coverage. This at least prompted action by the judge who then claimed the delay had been solely due to the fact that he had never been provided with a transcript. There was an implication that counsel had secreted the transcript in order to embarrass the court.

These examples, while extreme, are not isolated. Delays of up to one month between the submission of a case and the decision by the judge are common. Lawyers have been subjected to delays of weeks and months between submission of a case and a decision by the court.[40] Lawyers can't help thinking that the judge has forgotten the evidence by the time he writes his decision. No adequate remedy exists when there is an unreasonable delay on the part of a judge. He can be sued *in procedendo*, but this is expensive to the client and causes hard feelings on the part of the judge toward the lawyer handling the case. Repeated inquiries tend to irritate the judges, and thus lawyers and clients are reluctant to inquire about a decision for fear of irritating a judge and inducing an adverse decision. None of these problems arise when the case has been submitted to a jury.

The main claims are that a jury requires more time because: (1) the process of picking the jury (the *voir dire* examination of the jury) can be time consuming; (2) time is lost arguing over the admissibility of evidence which would not be required if the case were tried to a judge; and (3) final arguments by counsel are longer before juries than to judges. It has been suggested that the lawyers be limited in the questions they could ask jurors, and that most of the questioning should be done by the judge. This is the practice in many federal courts. The English practice is not to question jurors at all aside from those exceptional cases where there can be a preliminary showing of cause.

Any person who has observed the process of questioning

jurors by skillful counsel cannot doubt the value of *voir dire* in eliminating the eccentric, prejudiced and unqualified juror. Even prejudiced jurors who remain cannot help but be impressed with the fact that both sides are looking for fair and impartial jurors. Counsel who insist on wasting time should be brought into line by the court. The *voir dire* examination is often concluded within one-half hour and rarely exceeds two hours except in homicide cases. This is a small loss of time when the result is a fair jury. Kalven and Zeisel's work gave strong indications that *voir dire* was a valuable tool in obtaining a suitable jury.[41]

Time lost arguing over the evidence is mostly the fault of judges. Some judges, however, keep a tighter rein on evidence during jury trials, thereby shortening the trial.[42] Most objections require no argument, and a simple ruling by the judge suffices. Unique and novel questions do require argument and authority, but this is true even when there is no jury. Generally these questions can be anticipated and briefed or even decided in advance. The writer observed few objections in trials by English counsel in London, and in the United States, the more experienced the counsel, the fewer the objections. Highly qualified counsel do not object to even erroneous matters unless the objection will aid his cause.

Devlin[43] and Williams[44] claim the arguments of counsel are longer to juries than to judges sitting alone. It is granted that the length of the argument should have a reasonable relation to the length of the trial, the difficulty of the issues and the importance of the case to the litigants. Again, most arguments, even when no time is set by the judge, are about one-half hour for each side. It is not unusual for the arguments to be as short as 15 minutes or as long as 45 minutes. The court ought to be permitted, within reason, to limit argument. Most critics of summation arguments claim that these arguments serve no real purpose, but, in reality, they serve to condense into a short time what has usually taken at least two days. Argument brings the issues clearly into focus immediately before the jury begins deliberation. Counsel may well touch on the very matters that are decisive of the case, and, without this assistance, the jury may well miss the crucial points.

More distressing than the length of argument to juries is the practical elimination of argument in many courts when cases are tried to a judge alone. It is common for judges at the conclusion of the evidence to lean across the bench and ask, "Is there any need for argument?" The obvious implication is that counsel could not possibly say anything that could be of assistance in aiding the judge to reach a decision. The writer was once stopped by a judge even before argument. In a juvenile case, the judge, at the close of the state's evidence, directed this statement to the writer, "You can call your witnesses if you want to, but my mind's made up." The judge meant that his mind was made up in favor of the state without ever having heard the defense witnesses. The arrogance of judges in thinking that nothing can be said that will enlighten them is not mitigated by their supposition that juries share this obtuse quality.

The causes of court congestion are more deeply rooted than the delay inherent in a jury trial. Among the factors contributing to this congestion are increasing population, a greater frequency of accidents, and the failure of the public authorities to create new judgeships and court facilities.[45] Hung juries are often blamed for loss of time and delay, but inasmuch as it is usual for the cut and dried cased to be disposed of by settlement (in civil cases) and by guilty pleas (in criminal matters), it is not surprising to find that a large percentage of the more complex jury cases end in hung juries.[46] Hung juries, however, are not much of a problem, as most juries are generally able to reach a decision. As early as 1852, Forsyth observed that hung juries were not much of a problem,[47] and at Old Bailey in 1965 only 4.1 percent of the juries failed to reach a verdict. At the London Sessions, the percentage was even lower.[48] The rate of hung juries in America, according to Kalven and Zeisel, is about 5 percent,[49] and the writer's experience confirms these conclusions. In approximately 150 jury trials in which the writer has acted as counsel, only six ended in hung juries. Of these, the court and prosecution saw fit to retry only two, both of which ended in acquittals. The group nature of decision-making by a jury tends to soften the effect of radical and eccentric views.[50]

It would be ill advised, especially in criminal cases, to weaken the principle of unanimity inherent in a jury verdict,[51] merely to avoid the small chance of a hung jury. The requirement of unanimity "... insures that the case is proved beyond a reasonable doubt,"[52] and a mistrial due to disagreement is a "safeguard to liberty."[53] When you add to that the protection unanimity gives to minorities and the assurance that all important aspects of the case receive ample consideration,[54] it seems clear that the principle ought to apply to civil trials as well. Bear in mind that most civil and criminal cases are disposed of before trial. The experience of the writer also illustrates that the principle of unanimity tends to require a higher quantum of proof for a conviction in a criminal case. In all six cases in which there was a hung jury, there was no subsequent conviction.

It seems strange that judges themselves are not held to unanimity when trying cases in the first instance or on appeal. For instance, it is peculiar that an accused can be found to be guilty beyond a reasonable doubt by two judges when the third man holds him to be innocent. Those who believe judges are better able to correlate decisions with the true facts should become more aware of the disagreement among judges. The percentage of disagreement would no doubt run higher than the five percent rate of hung juries. This can be tested by thumbing through the decisions of the United States Supreme Court. *Johnson v. Louisiana*, 406 US 356, 92 Sup.Ct. 1620 (1972), is an outstanding example. This case produced seven different opinions, the majority opinion, two concurring opinions and four dissenting opinions. Chief Justice Vaughan commented on Bushell's case in 1670, "I would now whether anything be more common than for two students, barristers, or judges, to deduce contrary and opposite conclusions out of the same case in law."[55] As late as January, 1973, a prestigious New York Court held that a homosexual could be denied admission to the bar.[56] Where is the predictability in judge trial?

Some would try to save time by having smaller juries. One suggestion included the federal minijuries, noted earlier. The smaller jury diminishes the protection given to minorities, emphasizes the influence of a possible eccentric or dominant personality, and changes the nature of the decision making process. Any change in number should also be avoided purely because popular opinion would be opposed to it. In addition, reducing the number of challenges should go hand in hand with the reduction of size. In 1972 when Ohio reduced civil juries from 12 members to 8, the number of challenges was also reduced from four to three. Working with the larger number of jurors and challenges, attorneys have a better chance of getting rid of jurors who may not be fair. When the size of the jury is reduced from 12 to 8, however, the likelihood of a minority racial group being represented is substantially reduced, while the chances of the majority being represented are hardly affected at all. In addition, a change in the number of persons constituting a jury without a compelling reason tends to lower confidence in the results. Criminal jury trials average less than 35 per 100,000 population a year,[57] and even if the total number of jury trials were much larger, the jury's advantages justify its retention and keeping the jury at its present size.

The serious claim is made that juries are prejudiced, irrational and emotional. What trial lawyer would not occasionally find those same qualities in judges? It is said that male jurors favor a pretty woman; that juries won't convict of bootlegging, gambling and drunk driving; that they favor individuals over big corporations; and that they are prejudiced against minorities. Nearly all of these complaints have little significance when a jury is selected so as to be composed of both men and women, young and old and a true cross-section of the community. Generally, the jurors have no axe to grind, and certainly the more obvious cases of possible prejudice are eliminated during *voir dire* examination. An unfair juror who remains will, in a jury that is a true cross-section, be neutralized by a fair-minded majority.

As to the charge that juries nullify some laws and exercise the sovereign right of pardon, although having no explicit right to do so, the question must be asked whether this is not their real value. For example, although not all "drunks" are released, the jury may realize that alcoholism is not cured by a few days in jail, especially when this may result in the loss of the defendant's job. A partial answer to this and many other such situations may be to find a better remedy than jail.

An extreme example of the exercise of the power of pardon

is a case in which the writer was defense counsel. The defendant was charged with armed robbery. He was arrested for a crime in one jurisdiction which was committed only a few days after a very similar crime had been committed in another area. For the second crime he pleaded guilty and served over four years at hard labor. He was released, returned to Ohio on his own, became gainfully employed and worked for one year before he was arrested on the earlier charge. The jury was unable to reach a verdict the first time the case was tried. By the time the second case came on for hearing, the defendant had been in jail for about one year. The second robbery was admitted into evidence as a similar crime, an accomplice turned state's evidence, and the license number (except one digit was not available) of the car used in the first robbery was identical with the license of the defendant's automobile. The defendant's only defense was his denial and the testimony of close friends that he was in another state at the time of the robbery.

The jury returned a verdict of acquittal after four hours of deliberation. Whether the man was guilty or not, the writer, as is often the case, could not know for certain, although the evidence against the defendant was overwhelming. The jury no doubt concluded that four years served for another crime plus the year spent awaiting trial for the first robbery was sufficient punishment. The judge, on the other hand, thought the verdict was a miscarriage of justice. The defendant returned to his employment and several years later was still making his living at legal employment. If the judge had had his way, the defendant would still be in a penitentiary.

Another charge against the jury is that it is unpredictable. This could be acceptable, especially in civil cases, if it is assumed the cases are capable of being decided either way. This is always the situation in civil cases, unless the situation is such that the judge directs a verdict.

It is claimed that as to damages in personal injury cases, the size of the verdicts is especially difficult to anticipate. In view of the wide differential of not only the injuries and their consequences but also the varying backgrounds of the different parties, wide variations in the amount of the verdicts are to be expected. No doubt a board of doctors or judges would be capable of reducing the whole procedure to a formula which would allow specified amounts for named injuries, with variations only within narrow limits, without any attempt to make full compensation. In such a case the injured party would bear the greater part of the consequence of his injuries himself. Counsel who handle a fair number of personal injury cases, however, are able to predict within reasonable limits the verdicts of juries. There are publishing services which keep the lawyer informed of the latest results in personal injury cases, and, if the exceptional results are first eliminated, there is no undue variation. An examination of the exceptional cases often discloses exceptional circumstances which account for the results. On the other hand, however, you seldom hear that criminal cases are unpredictable. Experience seems to indicate that counsel can predict the jury's verdict about 90 percent of the time.

Another reason for preferring juries to judges is that, in criminal matters, juries really do require the state to prove their case beyond a reasonable doubt. This doubt is defined, in part, in some jurisdictions as an abiding conviction to a moral certainty of the truth of the charge. Kalven and Zeisel's study showed that the jury tolerates less doubt than judges. They concluded, "If society wishes to be serious about convicting only when the state has been put to proof beyond a reasonable doubt, it would be well advised to have a jury system."[58] A lower standard of proof could be adopted, but it would not seriously increase the total number which the judicial system holds responsible for crime. It must be remembered that the majority plead guilty. Many others are tried by judges who obviously don't use the reasonable doubt test, regardless of the law. Only a small percentage of all defendants are tried to juries, and some of these defendants are clearly innocent. Those who would lower the quantum of proof would do so for the sake of a few more convictions at the expense of some innocent persons being convicted.

Education of the public concerning the legal system is often listed as one of the advantages of the jury system.[59] De Tocqueville said of the jury:

It may be regarded as a gratuitious public school ever
open, in which every juror learns to exercise his
rights, enters into daily communication with the most
learned and enlightened members of the upper classes,
and becomes practically acquainted with the laws of
his country, which are brought within the reach of his
capacity by the efforts of the bar, the advice of the
judge, and even by the passions of the parties.[60]

Some persons have been heard to complain that jurors should
not be educated at the expense of the litigants. The same objection could be made against letting the masses vote, however.
Voters choose between candidates offering radically different
programs to the electorate, but far from restricting the electorate to an intellectual elite, the tendency has been to further
extend it until now in the United States almost any citizen of 18
or older can vote if he chooses. Our country has not suffered
from widely based suffrage or trial by jury. It has been argued in
the past and will continue to be argued that there are better
methods of government, but the people nonetheless prefer to
govern themselves, even if it results in a less efficient government.

The power of judgment has always been considered as a
part of the sovereign power of a nation. In deciding questions
between individuals, no more acceptable mode of decision has
ever been found than the submission of disputes to jurors. Experts, boards, and judges are not the "people." The jury ex-
ercises a portion of the sovereign power.[61] It is ultimately a belief based on intuition and instinct which requires that the
power of judgment in matters of the utmost consequence
should be by one's peers. A decision that 12 fellow citizens are
willing to live with has much to recommend it.

Jury trial ought, as a matter of policy, to be frequent
enough so that it is looked upon as the usual and preferred
mode of trial if not freely waived. If the jury is relegated to the
trial of exceptional cases only, it will be looked upon as an
anachronism instead of as mandatory for the maintenance of
justice and as a protection against arbitrary rule.[62] Frequency of
service resulted in knowledgeable jurors in classical Greece, for

example, and gave excellent results without setting undesirable precedents.[63] It is claimed that juries favor the poor,[64] but that is more desirable then the opposite alternative.

One line of criticism maintains that jury trial has a traumatic effect on some of the participants, particularly children who are parties or witnesses. There are children who have not obtained sufficient years to be capable of making coherent witnesses. There are even adults who are so emotionally disturbed as to be unable to deliver their testimony. For such instances, it ought to suffice to present their testimony by way of deposition. Actually, though, when children are too young to participate as a witness, their testimony would be of little value regardless of whether the trial was before a jury or otherwise.

The stress of trial is an important ingredient in obtaining truth. Many glib liars have gone undetected in the calm of an office deposition only to be exposed on the witness stand before a jury in the charged atmosphere of the courtroom. The greater part of legal tension is not due to the jury or the courtroom setting but to the importance of the matters in issue. Critics of jury trial, for example, would prefer to isolate otherwise intelligent teenagers from the court proceedings. However, if he suffers no physical or mental disability, there is no reason why he should not be allowed to give testimony in cases which pertain to him personally. In such cases as attempted institutionalization or child custody matters, it is dishonest not to allow the child to give his opinion in court, rather than to be restricted to the judge's chambers. As a matter of fact, the writer has called the children of persons accused of homicide to testify on their behalf, not for the sympathy effect but because they had facts to offer. They would have always regretted not giving their testimony if they had not been called, and the jury was never an impediment to their testifying.

It is said by some that the jury is inefficient because of the nature of the proceeding, the claim being made that there is no logical order to the evidence, that there are constant interruptions by counsel, that the schedule is inflexible, note taking is not permitted, the counsel make deliberate appeals to passion, and the jury is pressed for time in making a decision and cannot deliberate in private.

It is simply not true that there is no logical order to the evidence. Jury cases are generally opened by both sides outlining their cases to the jury. Of necessity, evidence is presented one word at a time, witness by witness. No one witness can cover the whole case in a single sentence. The preview by counsel helps the jury to understand the importance and relationship of each piece of evidence. The counsel also give much thought both to the order of witnesses as well as to the order in which questions are asked. The order chosen takes into consideration interest, chronology, similarity of subject matter and other matters. The overall effect most often shows a strong sense of organization.

If interruptions are too frequent, it can usually be attributed to the inexperience of counsel or the failure of the judge to keep control of the trial. Interruptions are not caused by the jury. The trial of a case involves, apart from the jury, counsel and parties for both sides, the judge and a number of witnesses. If a relatively inflexible schedule is adhered to, this is more suitable to the expedient disposition of the litigation, whether a jury is present or not. Also, continuances and extended adjournments are more common when there is no jury. This causes additional and repeated inconveniences to the parties, lawyers and witnesses, often for the mere personal convenience of the judge.

Some persons are convinced that note taking insures a better understanding of the evidence. On the other hand, someone once said that Cadmus (credited with importing 16 letters of the Greek alphabet from Phoenicia) did the human race a great wrong because reliance upon the written word weakens the powers of the mind. While this is an extreme view, observation of counsel tend to show that those who don't use notes make the most effective presentations. Some counsel go to the extreme of writing down almost everything said at trial. When the time comes for them to deliver their arguments, their counsel table is a clutter of papers and they hold in their hand an elaborate outline of their argument. Much of their time is wasted looking through their outline or going through the stack of notes, often without finding what they were looking for. The best impressions of a trial are overall impressions. If particular testimony is desired, the court reporter's transcript or electronic recording is more accurate than a juror's notes. Another difficulty with notes is that a person has difficulty doing more than one thing at a time, and thus both counsel and jurors who take notes are apt to miss important points of testimony. If a jury wrote down one piece of evidence, for example, that portion would receive undue emphasis.

As far as the claim that counsel appeals to the emotions of jurors, such appeals are often justified, although at other times such appeals should be stopped by the judge. Emotions are necessarily involved when livelihood, custody, freedom, reputation and fortune are at stake. Parties, lawyers and jurors and the law itself make a proper response to the emotions brought forth by the nature of the cause. It is passions which have nothing to do with the cause, such as racial prejudice, that should be stopped by the judge. Because of the emotional content necessary in a trial, however, the resolution of disputes can never be reduced to trial by computers.

If the jury was not pressed for a decision, they, like the judges, would procrastinate inordinately. Most cases are decided within a couple of hours, but when more time is required, jurors have enough fortitude and selflessness to take the time. As to deliberating in private, what is wanted is not 12 separate impressions but a joint verdict which is partially the result of group pressure. Little headway would be made toward a group decision if the jurors deliberated in private. Solitary deliberation would deprive the jurors of the recollections and inferences of fellow jurors.

Jury trials are of a higher quality than judge trials. Counsel have cases better prepared when the presentation is to a jury.[65] The notorious tendency of judges to hold preconceived ideas and to be impatient at the length of trial causes the lawyers to unnecessarily limit not only their arguments but the number of witnesses called and their preparation generally. Lawyers are at their best for jury trials. The cross-examination is more effective and more trouble is taken to have highly qualified experts present. When the trial is before the judge alone, the lawyer is apt to assume, rightly or wrongly, that the judge is a self-appointed expert in all fields and immune to any attempts to influence or change him. It is therefore not difficult for judge trials to resolve themselves into formalized traffic courts.

Plea trading is an interesting aspect of criminal trials. Kalven and Zeisel found that expectation of a lesser sentence if convicted by a judge than by a jury was a prime reason for waiver of trial by jury.[66] They also found that the waiver of a jury in a capital case was often tantamount to excluding the death penalty.[67] Any lawyer could have told them this, but what lawyers could not tell them is why there should be different penalties for identical crimes. One factor is that judges, despite what they say, don't like jury trials, preferring to take all trials to themselves. Thus, the innocent person who stands charged with a crime may be told by competent counsel that he runs a serious risk of conviction in view of the evidence against him, whether he is tried by the judge or the jury. At this point, the person with a criminal past would be more apt to opt for a judge trial and take advantage of the probability of obtaining a lighter sentence. The innocent victim of circumstances with a blameless background is more apt to choose the jury, being told, no doubt, that the quantum of proof the jury will require for conviction is higher than that which the judge would require. Upon conviction, therefore, the innocent person suffers a greater penalty than the guilty but more experienced criminal. This difference is totally the responsibility of judges who penalize litigants for choosing trial by jury.

The jury still relieves the judge from the responsibility of judging the most difficult cases, thereby diverting criticism from himself and his office,[68] justified or otherwise. The jury's verdict ensures that the verdict will be acceptable to a substantial portion of the community. It gives all adult citizens an opportunity to be self-governing even in judgment. The people believe in the jury system.[69] On top of all of this, Kalven and Zeisel have shown that the jury does understand the cases submitted to it, and, when it differs from what the judge might have decided, it does so for reasons of ultimate justice.[70]

If the jury is to be replaced, judges are usually suggested as the alternative.[71] A few observations about the quality of judges as an institution for obtaining justice should be pertinent. Even Judge Frank admitted:

> ... it is certain that we meet with judges who are at times harsher, more captious, more prone to convict, and at another more easy going, complaisant and more inclined to pardon.[72]

As a young lawyer, Judge Frank practiced before a distinguished judge who decided before hearing all of the evidence that a "... fine, hard working woman ought to win...," and so he ruled accordingly. This is not an uncommon example of a judge doing what juries are often accused of doing. At least in this case the jury would have been a representative portion of the sovereign.[73]

In many cases it has been found that judges do not follow the law if they can find a way to avoid it. Many jurisdictions formerly had statutory and constitutional provisions that permitted the jury to judge law as well as fact. Many judges paid scant attention to these enactments. An earlier author said of the judiciary's actions:

> What seems discreditable to the judiciary in the story which I have related is the fierce resolution and deceptive ingenuity with which the courts have refused to carry out the unqualified mandates of statutes and constitutional provisions.[74]

As far as the consistency of decisions by judges is concerned, the most damning study is that conducted under the direction of Charles Haines in 1915 and 1916 of the magistrates of New York City. According to his study, one judge, hearing cases of disorderly conduct, acquitted one defendant in 56.6 cases, while another acquitted 18 percent of the defendants, and another 54 percent.[75] He concluded:

> The tabulation of the statistician were prepared in part to discover the personal equation in the administration of justice and they showed that the magistrates differed to an amazing degree in their treatment of sim-

ilar classes of cases. The conclusion was inescapable that justice is a personal thing, reflecting the temperament, the personality, the education, environment, and personal traits of the magistrates. The results showing to what extent justice is affected by the personality of the judge were so startling and so disconcerting that it seemed advisable to discontinue the comparative tables of the records of the justices.[76]

A special commission of the New York Legislature was created to study the New York Court, and in 1973, according to press releases of January 6, it was found that there is still a great disparity in judicial decisions. For example, one judge might set bond at $500 in one case, while another judge would set bond at $5000 for an identical set of circumstances.

Lest the reader assume that the refusal of judges to follow the intent of legislative enactments is peculiar in America, attention is directed to the English courts. The Administration of Justice Act of 1933 provided:

Save as aforesaid [personal injury actions were not excepted], any action to be tried in that division [Queen's Bench] may, in the discretion of the court or a judge, be ordered to be tried either with or without a jury.

In 1937, the English Court of Appeals ruled that this enactment conferred an unfettered discretion on the judge to order a jury as he saw fit. In *Sims* v. *William Howard and Son, Ltd.*, 1964, 2 All English Reports 267, the same Court of Appeals held that the judges of the Queen's Bench had no discretion to order a jury trial in personal injury cases. Understandably, Justice Salmon, who concurred in the *Watts* case for reasons peculiar to the case, was unable to justify this strange reversal of a previous holding, especially in view of the clear language of the Act of Parliament.

These observations should be kept in mind by those who would eliminate the jury by creation of other tribunals or changing its basic nature. The only changes made in the jury system should be those which would strengthen its basic purposes. Computer selection of the panels chosen to report, programmed to give a true cross-section of the community, would be one such improvement. Also, this system could insure that jury service would be equitably spread among those available. The law ought to limit exemptions from duty to lawyers, judges, and court officials active in their profession and those with serious physical or mental disabilities. Excuses should be limited to those to whom jury service would be a real hardship, while those excused for a temporary reason should be reassigned to another panel.

In order to end a certain amount of hypocrisy in the system, a pamphlet ought to be given to all jurors setting forth their duties and a summary of the jury's history. In criminal cases the jury ought to be permitted to know what punishment the accused would be liable to upon a conviction. Even Judge Frank agrees that we should tell the jurors that they can decide contrary to the judge's charge if they find it necessary, even though the judge might not agree.[77] This has always been the practice in capital cases. In civil and criminal cases, jurors ought to be charged that under most circumstances they should take their law from the court but, in any event, they would not be required to return a verdict contrary to their consciences. The judge's charge ought to be brought into line with practice and theory. Frank looks upon the failure of the jury to follow the judge's charge as an act of legislation,[78] but in fact it is a solution suitable to a unique case. Legislation, on the other hand, applies generally to citizens and not to unique cases.

Other solutions are also feasible to increase the organization of the trial system. (1) Most civil cases should be tried to juries, including custody cases in divorce actions. Exceptions should be established for cases not having a certain jurisdictional amount, or, in the case of divorce, when there was no substantial property or custody question involved. (2) In complex cases the judge ought to be given authority to reduce the issue to a narrow one, capable of being resolved in a verdict in favor of one party or the other and/or for an amount of money. (3) There should be some adjustment from time to time in the jurisdictional amounts so that trials would be neither too burdensome nor too rare. (4) A citizen ought to be called for jury duty about every four years, and all cases should be concluded at the trial level within one year of filing and within two years at the appellate level. (5) Cases should be assigned according to specific criteria such as the order of filing, and thus both judge and jury trials would each be responsible for an equitable number of cases. (6) The judge ought to deliver a brief and generalized statement on the law and facts about which the law suit revolves at the beginning of the trial. (7) Jurors should be paid at least the average wage in the community plus expenses. In addition, the jury's purpose and history ought to be taught in all primary and secondary schools, so that all citizens would be able to understand the purpose and functioning of the jury system.

In conclusion, it should be noted that the public has great confidence in the jury, at least in the United States. Jury trial insures the common citizen of receiving very nearly the same justice as the others in society. The changing composition of the jury's membership from one trial to another avoids the frustration complex to which defeated clients and lawyers are susceptible, and protects judges from unfair criticism. When the jury is fairly representative of the community, it is the best protection against judicial injustice. But, the overriding reason for retaining and expanding the jury system is the belief that, given the benefits and dangers of any possible system of justice, the sovereign power of judgment ought to be vested directly in the people. We close with the words of DeTocqueville which are as true today as when they were written in the 1830's:

> He who punishes infractions of the law is therefore the real master of society. Now, the institution of the jury raises the people itself, or at least a class of citizens, to the bench of judicial authority. The institution of the jury consequently invests the people, or that class of citizens, with the direction of society.[79]

Chapter XI Footnotes

1. *Trial By Jury,* Sir Patrick Devlin (Stevens and Sons, 3rd ed., 1966), p. 147.
2. "Preservation of the Civil Jury," Stanley E. Sacks, 22 Wash. and Lee L. Rev. 76, 78 (1965).

3. *History of Trial by Jury*, William Forsyth (John W. Parker and Son, London, 1852), p. 15.

4. *Duncan v. Louisiana*, 391 U.S. 145 (1968).

5. *Williams v. Florida*, 391 U.S. 78, 107 (1970).

6. *Johnson v. Louisiana*, 406 U.S. 356, 92 Sup.Ct. 1620, 1652 (1972).

7. "The New Minijuries: Panacea or Pandora's Box?", David J. Gibbons, 58 A.B.A.J. 594 (June, 1972).

8. *Courts On Trial*, Jerome Frank (Princeton University Press, Princeton, New Jersey, 1949), p. 132.

9. "Civil Juries, Their Decline and Eventual Fall," Leon Sarky, 11 Loy. L. Rev. 243, 245 (1962-63).

10. "Juries as Judges of Criminal Law," Mark DeWolfe Howe, 52 Harv. L. Rev. 582 (1939).

11. *The Elements of the Art of Packing as Applied to Special Juries*, Jeremy Bentham (Effingham Wilson, London, 1821).

12. "General Observations on the Effect of Personal, Political, and Economic Influences In the Decisions of Judges," Charles Grove Haines, 17 Ill. Law. Rev. 96, 110 (1922).

13. *Commentaries On the Laws of England*, William Blackstone, Vol. 4 — 350 (1775).

14. *The Proof of Guilt*, Glanville Williams (Stevens and Sons, London, 3rd ed. 1963, 1st published 1955), p. 17.

15. "Address by the Right Honourable Lord Denning, Master of the Rolls," The Australian Law Journal, V 41, p. 224 (1967).

16. *A Historical Treatise On Trial By Jury*, Thorl. Gudn. Repp (Thomas Clark, Edinburgh, 1832), p. 103.

17. Forsyth, *op. cit.* at note 3, at p. 445.

18. *A History of English Law*, Sir William Holdsworth (Sweet and Maxwell, London, from 7th ed., 1956, reprinted 1966, 1st ed. 1903), V-1, p. 350.

19. Devlin, *op. cit.* at note 1, at p. 159.

20. *Middlemarch*, George Eliot (The Folio Society, London, 1972, first published 1871-2), p. 168.

21. Devlin, *op. cit.*, at note 1, at p. 149.

22. "The Case For The Retention Of The Unanimous Civil Jury," Howard Frank, 15 DePaul L. Rev. 403, 408 (1965).

23. "With Love In Their Hearts But Reform On Their Minds," 4 Col. J. of L. and Soc. Pro. 178, at 179 (1968).

24. *The Proof of Guilt, A Study of the English Criminal Trial,* Glanville Williams (Stevens and Sons, London, 3rd ed., 1st published, 1955), p. 325.

25. *The Jury,* W.R. Cornish (Penguin Press, London, 1968), p. 143.

26. *Id.,* at p. 160.

27. Cornish, *op. cit.,* at note 25, at p. 174.

28. Forsyth, *op. cit.,* at note 3, at p. 426.

29. Devlin, *op. cit.,* at note 1, at p. 159.

30. Holdsworth, *op. cit.* at note 18, at p. 349.

31. *Democracy In America,* Alexis Clerel DeTocqueville (George Adlard, New York, 3rd American Ed., 1839), footnote on p. 281.

32. Sarky, *op. cit.,* at note 9, at pp. 243, 255.

33. Cornish, *op. cit.,* at note 25, at p. 19.

34. Cornish, *op. cit., at note 25, at p. 265.*

35. "Abolition of the Civil Jury: Proposed Alternatives," Bruce Rashkow, 15 DePaul L. Rev. 417, 422 (1965).

36. *The American Jury,* Harry Kalven, Jr. and Hans Zeisel (Little, Brown and Company, Boston, 1960), p. 8.

37. Sacks, *op. cit.,* at note 2, at p. 83.

38. Sacks, *op. cit.,* at note 2, at p. 82.

39. Sacks, *op. cit.,* at note 2, at p. 83.

40. Sacks, *op. cit.,* at note 2, at pp. 83-4.

41. Kalven and Zeisel, *op. cit.,* at note 36, at pp. 295-96.

42. Sacks, *op. cit.,* at note 2, at pp. 83-4.

43. Devlin, *op. cit.* at note 1, at p. 145.

44. Williams, *op. cit.* at note 24, at p. 279.

45. Sacks, *op. cit.,* at note 2, at pp. 83-84.

46. Kalven and Zeisel, *op. cit.,* at note 36, at p. 31; Cornish, *op. cit.,* at note 25, at p. 31.

47. Forsyth, *op. cit.,* at note 3, at p. 249.

48. Cornish, *op. cit.* at note 25, at p. 258.

49. Kalven and Zeisel, *op. cit.* at note 36, at p. 453.

50. Kalven and Zeisel, *op. cit.*, at note 36, at p. 498.

51. Cornish, *op. cit.*, at note 25, at p. 145.

52. Williams, *op. cit.*, at note 24, at p. 315.

53. Kalven and Zeisel, *op. cit.*, at note 36, at p. 454.

54. Forsyth, *op. cit.*, at note 3, at p. 246.

55. *A Complete Collection of State Trials and Proceedings for High Treason,* Edited by T.B. Howell (T.C. Hansard, London, 1816), Vol. 6, p. 1006.

56. *The Wall Street Journal,* Editorial Page (January 19, 1973).

57. Kalven and Zeisel, *op. cit.* at note 36, at p. 498.

58. Kalven and Zeisel, *op. cit.* at note 36, at pp. 167, 181, 189.

59. Holdsworth, *op. cit.* at note 18, at p. 348; Cornish, *op. cit.,* at note 25, at p. 255; Williams, *op. cit.,* at note 24, at p. 282.

60. DeTocqueville, *op. cit.,* at note 31, at p. 284.

61. Detocqueville, *op. cit.,* at note 31, at p. 283.

62. DeTocqueville, *op. cit.,* at note 31, at p. 284

63. Frank, *op. cit.,* at note 8, at p. 221.

64. Devlin, *op. cit.,* at note 1, at p. 155.

65. Rashkow, *op. cit.,* at note 35, at p. 430.

66. Kalven and Zeisel, *op. cit.,* at note 36, at p. 26.

67. Kalven and Zeisel, *op. cit.,* at note 36, at p. 444.

68. Kalven and Zeisel, *op. cit.,* at note 36, at p. 7.

69. "With Love In Their Hearts But Reform On Their Minds," *op. cit.,* at note 23, at p. 188.

70. Kalven and Zeisel, *op. cit.* at note 36 at pp. 128, 495.

71. Kalven and Zeisel, *op. cit.* at note 36, at p. 9.

72. Frank, *op. cit.,* at note 8, at p. 163.

73. Frank, *op. cit.,* at note 8, at p. 168.

74. Howe, *op. cit.,* at note 10, at p. 616.

75. Haines, *op. cit.,* at note 12, at p. 105.

76. Haines, *op. cit.,* at note 12, at p. 105.

77. Frank, *op. cit.*, at note 8, at p. 137.

78. Frank, *op. cit.*, at note 8, at p. 137.

79. DeTocqueville, *op. cit.*, at note 31, at p. 282.

INDEX

References are to page numbers